"...(Ninth) printing
...Rare cookbook achievement..."
—Marie Ryckman, *Cincinnati Enquirer*

"Appetizers that say great party
...bridges a gap in the continuing flood of recipe collections..."
—Joanne Will, *Chicago Tribune*

"...300 very 'today' hors d'oeuvres..."
—Elizabeth Alston, *Redbook*

"Party foods for all occasions"
—John Stevens, *Ladies' Home Journal*

"...Hors d'oeuvres galore..."
—*Town and Country*

"...Familiar and...exotic ideas..."
—Helen McCully, *House Beautiful*

"Cincinnati book has chili secret
"...a godsend to many of the cooks who bought it."
—Cecily Brownstone, *Associated Press Food Editor*

"...Reviews many...all four star..."
—*Eat, Drink and Be Merry,* Robert J. Misch, *United Features Syndicate*

"One of the best"
—Lois Taylor, *Honolulu Star*

"...Everyone finds useful at party time"
—Elaine Tait, *Philadelphia Inquirer*

"...One of Cincinnati's most famous..."
—Joyce Rosencrans, *Cincinnati Post*

"...Family recipes...become best seller"
—Suzanne Holloway, *Tulsa World*

"All about appetizers"
—Helen Civelli Brown, *San Francisco Examiner*

"A must in cookbook collection..."
—Marguerite Lyons, (Lowell, Mass.) *The Sun*

"...Food editors...singing praises"
—Janet Burton, (Gary, Ind.) *Post-Tribune*

"Fund raiser best seller"
—Hazel Geisler, *St. Petersburg Independent*

"...Well organized...collection"
—Sandel English, (Tucson) *Arizona Daily Star*

"...A bible for entertaining"
—Joanne York (Eugene, Oregon) *Register Guard*

"...Whiz of a book
...stands out...within veritalbe mountain of new culinary reference material..."
—Susan Kreifel, *Lincoln* (Neb.) *Journal*

"...Excellent index..."
—Joan Goessl, *Milwaukee Journal*

"Elegance...without effort"
—Ann Collins, *Pensacola* (FL) *News*

"IN THE BEGINNING... living end
...a giant tour de force of the culinary kingdom of hors d'oeuvre."
—Ann Valentine, *Houston Post*

"Some mighty good ones

...200 pages...350 recipes...many...are very simple..."
—Bernie O'Brien, *Hollywood* (Fla.) *Sun Tattler*

"...Ultimate in hors d'oeuvre books"
—Jill Wolowic, *Columbus* (Ohio) *Dispatch*

"...Party planning...treasure..."
—Martha Giddens, *Savannah Morning News*

"...Hors d'oeuvre encyclopedia"
—Eileen Shepard, (Albany, N.Y.), *The Knickerbocker News*

"Perfect for holiday party season..."
—Nancy Weir, *Florida Times-Union*

"Become...queen of appetizer makers..."
—Patricia Coffey, *Bridgeport* (CT.) *Post*

"...Professionally done

...one cookbook I thoroughly enjoyed reviewing..."
—Kathy Adams, *Abilene* (Tx.) *Reporter-News*

"...Truly a goldmine of...ideas"
—Barbara Gibbs Ostman, *St. Louis Post-Dispatch*

"...Braille version...innovative recipes..."
—Rosemary Vavrin, *Anchorage* (Alaska) *Times*

We wish to express our appreciation to the news media for their splendid cooperation and encouragement.

IN THE BEGINNING

a collection of hors d'oeuvres

rockdale ridge press
8501 ridge road
cincinnati, ohio, 45236
513-891-9900

1st Printing — November, 1975
2nd Printing — January, 1976
3rd Printing — August, 1976
4th Printing — November, 1976
5th Printing — October, 1977
6th Printing — July, 1978
7th Printing — November, 1978
8th Printing — September, 1979
9th Printing — October, 1980

IN THE BEGINNING

Library of Congress Catloging in Publication Data

Main entry under title:

In the Beginning.

Includes index.
1. Cookery (Appetizers)
TX740.15   641.8'12   76-55355

Printed by
The Feicke Printing Co.
Cincinnati, Ohio

Typeset by
Reporter Typographics
Cincinnati, Ohio

ISBN 0-9602338-0-6

FOREWORD

To all hosts and hostesses everywhere who have dreamed of a cookbook comprised of hors d'oeuvres which are elegant to serve, but easy to prepare, IN THE BEGINNING is dedicated. Here are the finest hors d'oeuvres imaginable; they have brought raves from party givers and party goers.

We are grateful that so many shared prized recipes with us and with you. Some are original creations; others have been handed down from generation to generation. All are presented in a clear, concise, step-by-step manner. The end results are superb, only the preparations are simple.

From the time we first fancied the idea of a cookbook, we thought how exciting it would be to bring together in one handy volume all kinds of appetizers, canapes, soups and other hot and cold, delicate and hearty palate pleasers.

Now that fancy has become fact, we know that you'll agree that when it comes to hors d'oeuvres, IN THE BEGINNING is the living end!

ROCKDALE RIDGE PRESS

Cover Design and illustrations
by Alice H. Balterman

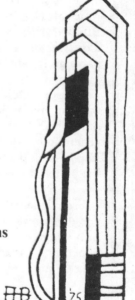

TO THE CONTRIBUTORS

IN THE BEGINNING is dedicated to the more than one hundred fine cooks whose prized and special recipes have been handed to us and to you on a silver platter.

Without them, without their generosity and their willingness to share, IN THE BEGINNING could not have had a beginning.

Their interest and their concern, their ingredients and their culinary talents served as the Genesis of this book.

We thank them through a dedication. It is our sincere hope that your pleasure in preparing and serving their treasures will multiply the dedication thousandfold.

THE EDITORS

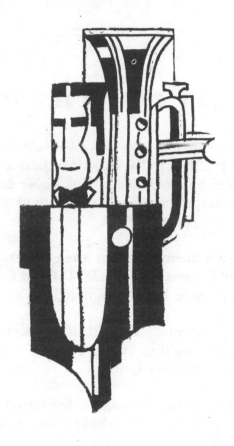

Braille Copies available on order from
National Braille Association

Braille Book Bank
422 Clinton Ave. S.
Rochester, N.Y. 14620

TABLE OF CONTENTS

TAKE A
REFRESHING
DIP

1

COLD DIPS

General Instructions for Cold Dips

Mix seasonings thoroughly with mayonnaise or sour cream. Let stand several hours in refrigerator before serving to blend flavors. May be prepared ahead and stored in covered container in refrigerator for several days.

Vegetables for Dipping

Asparagus	Cucumber slices
Radishes	Cherry tomatoes
Celery	Kohlrabi
Carrot strips	Cauliflower buds
Mushrooms	Broccoli buds
Pea pods	Turnip slices

Zucchini—Peel vegetable, cut crosswise in thirds, then cut like thick french fries and salt lightly with seasoned salt just before serving.

Filled Party Loaves

Crusty round French breads, round pumpernickels or long rye breads, hollowed out make great containers for dips. The loaf can be refilled when dip is used up. The bread is particularly delicious when soaked up with the dip. The loaf itself can be cut into chunks and served when it becomes empty.

1. To prepare loaf: Cut ¾" slice off top of loaf. Scoop out soft bread, leaving ¾" shell. Cut top slice and scooped out bread into cubes to use for dipping. (Wrap to prevent drying out.)
2. Place loaf on serving platter and fill loaf with desired dip. Garnish with caviar, parsley, paprika as desired. Place cubes of bread around loaf.

Note: A day old loaf is more easily handled.
   Loaf may be prepared ahead of time and stored in plastic bag in freezer or refrigerator

Suggested Combinations:

Pumpernickel bread
Beer Dip (page 14)
Hummus Bi Tahini (page 14)
Herring Dip (page 17)
Swiss Cheese Dip (page 23)
Creamy Fish Dip (page 17)

French or Vienna Bread
Cheese and Avocado Dip (page 15)
Olivacado Dip (page 15)
Thistle Dip (page 15)
Crabmeat Dip II or III (page 18)

Beer Dip

Serves 12

1 cup beer
1 pound sharp Cheddar
1¼ ounce pkg. Roquefort
2 tablespoons butter

½ medium onion
2 cloves garlic or
  1 teaspoon garlic powder
1 teaspoon Worcestershire
½ teaspoon Tabasco

1. Heat beer and cool.
2. Soften and cream together in mixer both cheeses and butter. Add the rest of the ingredients.
3. Use the beer to thin to spreading consistency.

Hummus Bi Tahini
(Chick Peas with Sesame Seed Paste)

Serves 12-15 people

1 pound can chick peas
Juice of 4-6 lemons, to taste
4-6 cloves garlic, crushed
1 teaspoon salt
1 cup tahini (sesame seed paste)
1 round rye, pumpernickel or
potato bread, unsliced

Garnish:
2 tablespoons olive oil
2 teaspoons paprika
2 tablespoons finely chopped
  parsley
10 whole chick peas

1. Drain chick peas. Put aside about 10 for garnish.
2. In electric blender, pour in lemon juice and a few drops of water. Add tahini, garlic and salt. Blend at high speed adding chick peas, a few at a time, until it reaches a consistency of a cream paste. If paste remains too thick, add water or lemon juice, a little at a time. Adjust seasoning (lemon, garlic, salt).

Note: Hollow bread. Pour hummus mixture into bread and garnish by dribbling olive oil mixed with paprika over surface of hummus. Sprinkle with chopped parsley and arrange a decorative pattern of whole chick peas on top. Cut hollowed out bread into serving cubes to be used for dipping into hummus mixture.

Note: The tahini, or sesame paste, can be purchased in any Greek food store. The paste is made from sesame meal. This recipe is most widely known and appreciated in the Middle East.

Cheese and Avocado Dip

Serves 12

1-8 ounce can whipped creamed
   cheese
1 ripe avocado
½ cup mayonnaise

Juice of ½ lemon
Pinch of garlic powder

1. Beat together creamed cheese, mashed avocado, mayonnaise, lemon juice and garlic powder. Paprika may be sprinkled on top.

Suggestion: Can be made same day and put in refrigerator. Everyone raves about it.

Olivacado Dip

1 ripe avocado
1-2½ ounce can sliced or
   chopped ripe olives

½ teaspoon seasoned salt
Juice of ½ lemon or lime
1 tablespoon grated fresh onion

1. Remove flesh from avocado by scooping from skin with spoon. Save shell to use for heaping back into it the following mixture:
2. Mix flesh with olives drained well, onion, seasoned salt and lime or lemon juice.
3. Heap back into avocado shells.

Note: Serve with crisp slices of fresh carrot, turnip, radish, kohlrabi or other fresh vegetables. (Worth trying unusual ones.)

Thistle Dip

Makes 1½ cups

1-6 ounce jar marinated
   artichoke hearts
1 cup sour cream

½ teaspoon onion salt
Dash cayenne pepper

1. Place artichokes with liquid in blender. Cover and blend, scraping down sides as needed until completely smooth.
2. Transfer to bowl. Stir in remaining ingredients.
3. Refrigerate at least 1 hour.

Note: Serve with crackers, potato chips, or vegetables.

Spinach Dip

1 package frozen, chopped
   spinach
½ cup chopped scallions
½ cup finely minced parsley
2 cups Hellman's mayonnaise
   (Do not use any other brand)

1 teaspoon salt
⅛ teaspoon freshly ground
   pepper

1. Thaw spinach and squeeze out liquid.
2. Mix all ingredients together and chill for 24 hours.

Note: Excellent with raw vegetables."One of the best vegetable dips."

Spinach Nancy

1 package of frozen,
   chopped spinach
2 tablespoons mayonnaise

Pinch garlic salt
⅛ teaspoon red pepper
½ teaspoon lemon juice

1. Cook and drain spinach as directed on package.
2. Mix with remaining ingredients and season to taste.

It's easy! Folks like it. Make a day ahead. Serve in small bowl surrounded with small crackers or party rye.

Pesto Leonardo

2/3 cup fresh basil leaves
1/3 cup fresh flat Italian parsley
½ cup olive oil
½ cup Parmesan, fresh grated
1/3 cup Pignoli (pine nuts)

4 cloves garlic, minced
1 teaspoon fresh grated black
   pepper
1 cup Ricotta cheese

1. Chop parsley and basil a little. Put in blender with 2 tablespoons olive oil and garlic. Blend until you have a green paste.
2. Add pine nuts and 2 tablespoons more of the olive oil. Blend 2 minutes Add remaining ingredients and blend until smooth and well mixed.

Not for the fainthearted!

A spicy dip for vegetables or crackers.

Make in summer using fresh basil.

Freezes well.

Serve as a sauce for pasta. Warm but do not boil. Serve over Fettucini or Cavatelli. Top with grated Romano.

Herring Dip

1-12 ounce jar herring
2 tablespoons dehydrated onion
2 teaspoons sugar

1 pint sour cream
2 teaspoons mustard seed
½ cup chopped tart
  apple

1. Drain herring on paper towels.
2. Chop herring and mix with remaining ingredients.

Make a day ahead.

Creamy Fish Dip

1 pound jar gefilte fish
  in liquid broth
3 tablespoons fish broth
1 teaspoon lemon juice

2 teaspoons prepared white
  horseradish
½ teaspoon salt
Dash pepper

1. Drain fish, reserving broth.
2. Blend fish with remaining ingredients in blender.
3. Refrigerate for about one hour.

Note: Serve with crackers.

Green Goddess Dip

Serves 6

1 clove garlic, minced
1—2 ounce can anchovies,
  chopped
3 tablespoons chopped chives
  (dried or fresh)
1 tablespoon vinegar

½ cup sour cream
1 cup mayonnaise
1/3 cup chopped parsley
  or
3 tablespoons dehydrated parsley

Put all ingredients in the blender and blend till smooth. (A little milk may be added if it seems to be too thick).

This dip is fantastic when served with fresh cut-up vegetables. If there is any left over, use it as a salad dressing. It may be made a day or two ahead and refrigerated.

Crabmeat Dip I

Serves 6

1 cup smooth cottage cheese
1 teaspoon Worcestershire
½ teaspoon MSG
2 teaspoons dill weed
* 1 can crabmeat
2 tablespoons buttermilk

1 tablespoon lemon juice
½ teaspoon salt
Fresh ground pepper
2 teaspoons mustard seed
¼ cup chopped, drained cucumber

1. Combine all ingredients, adding more buttermilk if necessary to obtain good consistency.
2. Correct seasonings. Makes 2¼ cups.

A good low calorie dip.

Crabmeat Dip II

Serves 12 or so

1 pint sour cream
1 package onion soup mix

* 1-7½ ounce can crabmeat

1. Pick shell and bones from crab meat.
2. Mix together with cream and soup mix till well blended.

Should be made several hours ahead and chilled. Serve with crackers or potato chips.

Crabmeat Dip III

* 2-6 ounce boxes frozen Alaska
   King Crab
½ cup Hellman's mayonnaise

½ cup sour cream
½ cup chopped celery

1. Thaw crab. Mix with remaining ingredients.

Serve with crackers or party rye. Make as much as you can afford. It won't be left over!

*(See page 26)

18

Shrimp Dip I

Serves 16

1-8 ounce package
  cream cheese
1 cup tomato catsup
2 tablespoons grated onion

½ teaspoon prepared mustard
½ to ¾ pound shrimp, cut up
Tabasco, salt & paprika
  to taste

1. Soften cheese and combine all ingredients in electric blender.
2. Chill.

Serve with melba toast.

Shrimp Dip II

Serves 4

1-3 ounce package cream cheese
½ dozen shrimp, cut fine
3 tablespoons cocktail sauce

Dash A-1 sauce
Salt and pepper to taste

1. Cream cheese till soft (add a little milk). Mash in shrimp.
2. Add cocktail sauce, A-1 sauce, salt and pepper. Blend until proper consistency to spread (adding milk or more cocktail sauce).

Can be made ahead. Use crackers or vegetables for dipping.

Sour Cream Shrimp Dip

Makes 1½ cups

1-5 ounce can shrimp, drained
1 cup sour cream
¼ cup chili sauce
2 teaspoons lemon juice

½ teaspoon salt
⅛ teaspoon pepper
1 teaspoon horseradish
Dash Tabasco sauce

Cut shrimp into small pieces and mix with other ingredients.

Note: Use as a spread or dip.

Shrimp Cheese Dip

Makes about 2 cups

¼ cup milk
½ cup mayonnaise
1-5 ounce can shrimp, drained
1 small onion, cut up

1 cup cubed Cheddar cheese
1 tablespoon Worcestershire
¼ teaspoon garlic salt
3 drops hot pepper sauce

1. Put all ingredients in a blender and blend until smooth.
2. Chill.

Serve with crackers to dip.

Provencal Canapé Spread (or Dip)

Serves 6

4 tablespoons mayonnaise
2 tablespoons oil (olive or
vegetable or half of each)
1 tablespoon prepared mustard
(mild)
1 medium Spanish onion,
finely chopped

10 anchovy fillets, finely chopped
2 hard boiled eggs, finely chopped
1 lemon (juice and rind)
Freshly ground black pepper

Serve on buttered round of
Italian bread

1. Combine and beat until smooth the mayonnaise, oil and mustard.
2. Add remaining ingredients (may not need all the lemon juice;
therefore, add this as needed for taste and consistency).

*A very delicately flavored dish which should not be overwhelmed by
savory breads. This can be served as a dip, with Devonshire Toasts.*

Pink Devil Dip

Makes 1 cup

1 cup sour cream
2 tablespoons bottled chili sauce
¼ teaspoon prepared horseradish

1-4 ounce can deviled ham
1 teaspoon instant minced onion

1. Combine all ingredients in a small bowl and stir to blend well.
2. Cover and chill one hour.

Serve as a dip with potato chips or corn chips.

Surprise Dip

Serves 10-12

1 can tomato soup,
undiluted
Dash of Tabasco sauce
Dash of onion powder

½ cup mayonnaise
Dash of Worcestershire sauce
Dash of garlic powder

1. Mix all ingredients together well.

Serve with potato chips or as a salad dressing.

Tastes like a cheese dip; most guests can't guess the ingredients.

Quick Dips

Caviar Dip

8 ounces sour cream

Small jar caviar

Curry Dip I

1 cup mayonnaise

Curry powder, to taste,
(1 to 3 teaspoons)

Curry Dip II

1 cup mayonnaise
1 tablespoon tarragon vinegar
1 teaspoon horseradish

1 teaspoon dehydrated onion
1 teaspoon garlic salt
1 teaspoon curry powder

Nippy Dip

1 cup sour cream
3 cups Hellman's mayonnaise
2 tablespoons chopped
  capers, drained
½ cup frozen chopped chives

1 clove garlic, crushed
½ cup chopped parsley
  (or 2-3 tablespoons dehydrated)
1 teaspoon Tabasco sauce
1 to 3 teaspoons horseradish,
  to taste

A Quick Dip

1 cup mayonnaise

1½ teaspoon Tarragon vinegar

Onion Soup Dip

1 package onion soup mix
1 pint sour cream

1. Blend contents of onion soup mix with sour cream.
2. Chill.

Note: This is one of the oldest of dips. It is tasty and easy for emergencies. Serve surrounded by potato chips or vegetables for dipping.

Vegetable Dip

1 cup sour cream
1 cup mayonnaise
2 tablespoons Beau Monde
  seasoning

1 tablespoon dill weed
1 teaspoon grated onion
  (optional)
1 teaspoon parsley

1. Combine all ingredients, blending thoroughly.

Serve as a dip with assorted vegetables.

Tangy Clam Dip

1 can New England Clam Chowder (undiluted)
2 heaping tablespoons minced onions

2 tablespoons catsup
8 ounces cream cheese
½ teaspoon horseradish

1. Put into blender until smooth.

Refrigerate until ready to use. Serve with chips, celery, or cauliflower.

Tomato Clam Dip

Makes 2 cups

1 pint sour cream
1-7½ ounce can minced clams, drained

1½ ounce envelope spaghetti sauce mix

1. Combine all ingredients in a small bowl and blend well.
2. Cover and chill one hour.

Serve as a dip with potato chips or crackers.

Low Calorie Clam Dip

Serves 6

1½ cups smooth cottage cheese
1 tablespoon lemon juice
¼ teaspoon grated onion
½ teaspoon Accent

1-2 teaspoons clam juice
1-2 tablespoons buttermilk
Salt & pepper to taste
1-7½ ounce can well drained minced clams

1. Combine all ingredients, adding enough liquid to obtain good consistency.
2. Correct seasonings.

Serve with vegetables for dipping.

Clam Dip

Makes 1¼ cups

1-7 ounce can minced clams
½ teaspoon finely diced onion
½ teaspoon salt

⅛ teaspoon pepper
2-3 ounce packages cream cheese, broken in pieces

1. Drain clams, reserving broth.
2. Put onion, clams, 2 tablespoons clam broth, seasonings and cream cheese in blender. Cover, blend till just mixed.
3. Chill before serving.

Note: Can be made ahead. Serve with carrot sticks, celery or potato chips.

Yogurt Vegetable Dip - Low Calorie

Makes 1 cup

½ cup smooth cottage cheese
1 tablespoon finely grated carrot
2 teaspoons finely grated onion
1 teaspoon finely grated
  green pepper

½ teaspoon salt
⅛ teaspoon garlic salt
Dash white pepper
1 cup plain yogurt

1. Beat cottage cheese in a small bowl, using a fork.
2. Add remaining ingredients, except yogurt, and mix well.
3. Fold in yogurt, cover and chill.

Serve with raw vegetables and chips.

Herb Yogurt Dip - Low Calorie

Makes 1 cup

1 teaspoon caraway seeds
1 tablespoon chopped green onion

1 cup plain yogurt
¼ teaspoon basil leaves,
  crushed

1. Pour boiling water over caraway seeds and let stand 5 minutes, then drain.
2. To yogurt, add caraway seeds, green onion and basil.
3. Chill several hours.

Serve with raw vegetables.

Swiss Cheese Dip

½ cup mayonnaise
2 tablespoons chili sauce
1 cup creamed cottage cheese
1 small wedge onion, chopped

¼ teaspoon salt
¼ teaspoon celery salt
1 cup cubed Swiss cheese

1. Place all ingredients, except Swiss cheese, in blender. Blend on high until smooth.
2. Add cheese a little at a time until blended.

HOT DIPS

Chili Con Queso

Serves about 8

1 pound American cheese
1-4 ounce can diced green chilies
1 pound can whole tomatoes
1 tablespoon diced minced onions

1. Cut cheese into small cubes.
2. Drain tomatoes and then chop fine; reserve liquid.
3. Add all ingredients to a chafing dish or double boiler and heat to melt cheese and mix ingredients. Adjust thickness using reserved tomato juice to give smooth dip consistency. Add more chilies if hotter taste is desired.

For fire eaters the whole can of green chilies can be used. Otherwise, start with no more than ¼-½ can of chilies (balance can be frozen.)

Can be made ahead. Serve hot from chafing dish with corn chips (tortilla chips.)

Hot Brie

Serves 16-20

*1 whole Brie cheese, well-ripened (2 pounds)
1 cup slivered almonds.

1. Place cheese in oven-proof serving dish. Sprinkle almonds over top.
2. Bake in 300° oven for 20 minutes (until cheese is soft and almonds brown).

Serve with assorted crackers. A delectable delight.

Easy elegance.

*A whole small canned Brie may be substituted. Use 1/3 cup almonds and reduce baking time to 15 minutes.

Hot Crabmeat Dip

½ pound Velveeta cheese   * 1-7½ ounce can crabmeat
½ cup (one stick) butter or margarine   Sherry

1. Melt cheese and butter in top of double boiler. Stir hard until blended.
2. Mix in drained crabmeat and enough Sherry to give spreading consistency.

Note: Serve in chafing dish with crackers.

Hot Crab Spread

* 2-6 ounce packages frozen or
  2-7½ ounce cans crabmeat, drained
1 pound cream cheese
½ cup mayonnaise
1 bunch green onions, chopped

2 dashes hot red pepper sauce
1 teaspoon Worcestershire sauce
Handful of slivered almonds

1. Mix all together, reserving almonds for topping.
2. Place in bake-and-serve dish and bake at 350° for 20 minutes.

Note: Serve with crackers.

Hot Crabmeat Soufflé Dip

* 1-7½ ounce can crabmeat, drained
1-8 ounce package cream cheese
1 teaspoon horseradish

8 ounce container sour cream
Pinch of sugar
lemon juice to taste

1. Flake crabmeat and add to softened cream cheese. Mix with other ingredients.
2. Bake ½ hour at 350° in soufflé dish.

*

> *SUGGESTIONS FOR PREPARING CRABMEAT*
> *For crab dishes using canned or frozen crab, pick it over carefully for pieces of bone and shell.*

Casa Pecan Spread

1-8 ounce package cream cheese, softened
2 teaspoons milk
1 jar (2½ ounce) sliced, dried beef
¼ cup finely chopped green peppers
2 tablespoons dehydrated onion flakes
½ teaspoon garlic salt
½ teaspoon pepper
½ cup dairy sour cream
½ cup coarsely chopped pecans
1 tablespoon margarine
½ teaspoon salt

1. Combine softened cream cheese and milk, mixing until well blended.
2. Stir in dried beef, onion flakes, green peppers and seasoning; mix well. Fold in sour cream.
3. Spoon into 8 inch pie plate or small baking dish.
4. Heat and crisp pecans in melted butter or margarine and salt. Sprinkle over cheese mixture.
5. Bake at 350° degrees for 20 minutes.

Serve hot with crackers. Can be assembled the night before and refrigerated. Bake when ready to serve.

Note: Casserole should be at room temperature before placing in oven to prevent cracking.

Hot Shrimp Dip

1 can cream of shrimp soup
1-5 ounce can shrimp
1-4 ounce can mushrooms cut into pieces (drained)
1 tablespoon Parmesan cheese
1 teaspoon Worcestershire sauce
1 tablespoon chopped parsley

1. Mix all ingredients together.
2. Heat in saucepan.

Note: Serve in small fondue pot with melba rounds.

FONDUES

Suggestions for Fondues

1. Two types of cheese used in fondues are Emmentaler and Gruyére. Emmentaler is milder and is used for a mild tasting fondue. Half Emmentaler and half Gruyére can be used for a stronger tasting fondue and Gruyére cheese alone makes the strongest flavor. Use a well-aged cheese to prevent stringy fondue.
2. The cheese melts more smoothly when cut into very small pieces or shredded, not grated.
3. The type of wine used is important. It should be light, lively, dry white wine such as Chablis, Riesling, Neuchatel or Rhine. If the wine is not tart enough, add a little lemon juice, about 1½ teaspoons for every half pound of cheese.
   Kirsch (cherry brandy) is the most popular liqueur used in making fondue, but brandy, cognac, light white rum or apple jack may be used or the liqueur omitted.
4. Keep mixture bubbling lightly.
   If the fondue gets too thick while being served add a little wine that has been warmed first. If it separates or gets lumpy, put the fondue back on the stove and stir in ½ teaspoon cornstarch blended with a little warm wine, then stir with a whisk until smooth.
5. Spear bread chunks on fondue fork and dunk with stirring motion.
6. A pottery fondue pot is the best type of container as it produces an even heat and prevents curdled and stringy fondue.

Cheese Fondue

Serves 6 to 8

1½ pounds Emmentaler,
  shredded
4 tablespoons flour
3 cups dry white wine
2 cloves of garlic, peeled
  and cut in half
½ teaspoon salt

Pinch white pepper
Dash nutmeg
2 tablespoons Kirsch,
  brandy or cognac
Bite-sized pieces of
  French bread

1. Dredge cheese with flour.
2. In a metal or Corning Ware sauce pan, put in wine and set over low heat. Heat till bubbles rise to surface (Important: do not let wine reach boiling point) and stir with a wooden spoon or fork or silver fork.
3. Add cheese, little at a time, while continuing to stir. Keep stirring until mixture is bubbling lightly.
4. Rub bottom and sides of an earthenware 2-quart casserole or fondue pot with garlic clobes. Set on heating element.
5. Add seasonings and Kirsch to cheese mixture; blend well and pour into casserole.

For onion-cheese fondue: Add 1 envelope (1⅜ ounces) dry onion soup mix to wine before heating. Omit salt, pepper and nutmeg.

Cheddar Cheese Fondue

Makes 2 cups

¼ cup butter or margarine
¼ cup flour
1 teaspoon MSG
½ teaspoon salt
¼ teaspoon dry mustard
1 can (12 ounces) beer

1½ teaspoons Worcestershire
2 cups (½ pound) shredded
  sharp Cheddar cheese
Bite-size pieces
  pumpernickel bread

1. Melt shortening in saucepan and blend in flour, MSG, salt and dry mustard.
2. Slowly add beer and Worcestershire.
3. Cook, stirring constantly, until mixture thickens and comes to a boil.
4. Add cheese; cook, stirring constantly, until melted.
5. Keep warm in a fondue dish.

Serve with chunks of pumpernickel bread speared on forks.

Bacon and Cheese Fondue

Makes 1½ cups

4 slices bacon, cooked, drained
   and crumbled
1 can (8 ounce) tomato
   sauce with onions
⅛ teaspoon garlic salt

⅛ teaspoon pepper
½ cup shredded Cheddar
   cheese
Bite size pieces of
   French bread

1. Combine bacon and tomato sauce, garlic salt and pepper and simmer for 5 minutes.
2. Add cheese, stirring constantly until melted and smooth.

Serve in fondue dish, with chunks of French bread for dunking.

Swiss Cheese Fondue

Serves 8

1 clove garlic
1 cup Chablis, or any dry white wine
1 pound Swiss cheese,
   grated

1 tablespoon cornstarch mixed
   with little water
1 ounce Kirsch liqueur

1. Rub earthenware fondue pot or pyrex dish with garlic.
2. Place pot over burner, pour in wine and warm it.
3. Add grated cheese. Stir constantly with wooden spoon until cheese melts.
4. Add cornstarch water to cheese, stirring constantly until thickened.
5. Before serving add Kirsch.

Note: Serve in chafing dish or fondue dish with French bread cubed, toasted and speared on a fork to dip in fondue.

SPREADING JOY

2

CHEESE BALLS AND LOGS

Use your imagination in shaping these cheese mixtures. But remember, once guests start digging in, the log stays neater than the ball.

Cheese Log

1 pound sharp Cheddar, shredded
1 cup chopped pecans
Chili powder

1-8 ounce package cream cheese
1 clove garlic, mashed

1. Have cheeses at room temperature. Blend with pecans and garlic.
2. Make into 2 rolls, about the diameter of a silver dollar. Roll in chili powder on a piece of waxed paper until heavily coated.
3. Chill.

Serve with assorted crackers.
May be made ahead and either refrigerated or frozen.

Bleu Cheese Ball

1-3 ounce package cream cheese
1-3 ounce package cream cheese with chives
2 ounces Bleu cheese

⅛ cup butter
1/3 cup drained chopped black olives
½ cup chopped nuts

1. Soften cheeses and butter, mix with olives, and chill.
2. Shape into ball and roll in chopped nuts.

Salmon Party Log

1 pound can salmon
¼ teaspoon salt
3 tablespoons snipped parsley
2 teaspoons grated onion
1 cup chopped pecans

8 ounces cream cheese, soft
¼ teaspoon Liquid smoke
1 tablespoon lemon
1 teaspoon horseradish

1. Drain salmon well. Bone and flake.
2. Combine everything except parsley and nuts. Chill several hours.
3. Roll in log (heavy wax paper helps).
4. Roll log in nuts and parsley, or just in parsley.

Serve with party rye bread.
Keeps in refrigerator for days.

Cheese-Olive Roll

½ pound Bleu cheese
1-8 ounce package cream cheese
¼ cup butter
1 tablespoon minced
   chives

1 tablespoon brandy
½ cup minced ripe olives
Chopped toasted almonds

1. Cream together Bleu cheese and cream cheese with butter.
2. Add chives, brandy and minced ripe olives.
3. Form mixture into a roll, cover with almonds and chill.
4. Slice and serve with toasted crackers.

Roquefort Cheese Ball

4 ounces Roquefort
1-6 ounce package sharp
   Cheddar cheese
3 ounces cream cheese
1 teaspoon MSG
1-2 teaspoons onion salt

½ teaspoon Worcestershire
   sauce
¾ cup finely chopped nutmeats
   (preferably walnuts)

1. Allow cheeses to stay at room temperature to soften.
2. Mix with seasonings and ½ cup nutmeats; blend well.
3. Place mixture on wax paper and shape into a ball.
4. Refrigerate for 1-2 hours and then roll ball in the remaining ¼ cup nutmeats.

Refrigerate until one hour before serving time. Use as a spread on crackers or icebox rye.

Mystery Cheese Ball

Makes 3 cheese balls

2 pounds Old English cheese, shredded
5 ounce jar Bleu cheese spread
8 ounces cream cheese
Chopped nuts or parsley

1. Leave cheese at room temperature and then blend in electric mixer.
2. Shape into 3 large balls. Roll in chopped nuts or parsley.

Will feed an army!

May be frozen.

Serve at room temperature.

Zingy Ham Butter Ball

Makes 5" ball

3 tablespoons dehydrated
  bell pepper
1/3 cup tarragon vinegar
3 tablespoons Mei Yen
  seasoning (Spice Island)
2 tablespoons dry mustard

2 sticks butter
2½ tablespoons onion
  powder
1 cup (8 ounces) ground ham

1. Soak bell peppers in vinegar for 15 minutes.
2. Cream together butter and seasonings.
3. Grind ham. Mix with all above ingredients.
4. Form into ball.

Make ahead. Keeps several days.

Cream Cheese Beef Log

Serves 6 to 8

1-8 ounce cream cheese
1/3 cup Parmesan cheese

1/3 cup chopped olives
1 package (3 ounces) chipped
  beef

1. Combine all ingredients except beef, mixing well.
2. Chop beef into small pieces.
3. Roll cheese into log shape.
4. Roll cheese log in beef pieces, covering well.

The chipped beef is a nice change. Make a day ahead - serve with assorted crackers.

Aunt Florence's Crabmeat Log

6-8 servings

8 ounces cream cheese
* 1 can crabmeat
1 bottle chili sauce

Dash Tabasco
Parsley—either fresh chopped
or dried

1. Soften cream cheese and mash down to ⅛ to ¼" thick in shape of a circle on serving plate.
2. Pick over well-drained crabmeat and make sure all hard pieces of shell, etc. are removed. Break up into flakes and sprinkle in a thick layer over cream cheese.
3. Drain chili sauce of extra liquid and add dash of Tabasco and mix. Pour mixture on cream cheese and crabmeat layers.
4. Cover with parsley so that the red layer is covered by a green layer.
5. Take 4 paper napkins, roll each up in roll to catch liquid which will drain. Allow hors d'oeuvre to drain with napkins in place until ready to serve.
6. Remove napkins and serve with crackers.

Cheese-Ball Hors d'oeuvre

Makes 1-2 lb. cheese balls

2-8 ounce packages
  sharp Cheddar cheese
2-8 ounce packages American
  cheese
2-3 ounce packages cream cheese
2 tablespoons Worcestershire sauce

1 teaspoon hot pepper sauce
2 large cloves garlic, pressed
1 tablespoon chili powder
1 tablespoon paprika

1. Grate Cheddar and American cheese in mixing bowl, blend cheeses together. Work together until there are no lumps.
2. Add Worcestershire sauce, hot pepper sauce and garlic. Blend.
3. Place in refrigerator until firm enough to form one large or two smaller balls. Roll the ball in the chili powder and paprika that have been mixed together.

Store in refrigerator, wrapped in wax-paper, until ready to serve. It will keep fresh for a week. Place on larger platter. Tuck parsley or watercress around base of ball. Surround by assortment of crackers.

* (See page 26)

Tomato-Cheese Log

Serves 10

1/3 cup tomato paste
8 ounces cream cheese,
  softened
8 ounces Cheddar cheese, grated
½ cup butter or margarine

2 tablespoons dehydrated
  chopped onion
2 cloves garlic, crushed
1 teaspoon salt
⅛ to ¼ teaspoon cayenne pepper
8 ounces chopped walnuts

1. Combine all ingredients except walnuts; beat with electric mixer until smooth.
2. Spoon out onto a large piece of wax paper. Roll with wax paper to form log.
3. Place in freezer one hour or until firm.
4. Cover with chopped walnuts.
5. Place on platter and serve as an appetizer.

Keep in refrigerator until ready to serve.

Can be made ahead. Serve very cold.

Stuffed Edam Cheese

1 Edam cheese (7-8 ounces)
¼ cup butter
½ teaspoon dry mustard
Dash Tabasco

¼ cup chopped green olives
2 teaspoons minced
  dehydrated onion
2 teaspoons dry wine
2 teaspoons caraway seed

1. Cut top from Edam cheese. Scoop out inside and blend with remaining ingredients.
2. Pack back into shell.

Serve with crackers or ice box rye. The red wax shell makes a colorful container. No dish to wash.

For easier handling: Remove celophane while cheese is cold. Leave at room temperature for several hours before trying to scoop cheese out of wax shell.

SPREADS

Crab Meat Spread or Shrimp Spread

Serves 12

2-8 ounce packages
  cream cheese
1 small onion diced very fine
½ cup mayonnaise
1 tablespoon lemon juice
1 teaspoon garlic salt

1 tablespoon Worcestershire sauce
½ bottle chili sauce
* 1-6 ounce box frozen crab meat
  or 1 package small frozen
  cooked shrimp

1. Soften cream cheese at room temperature.
2. Add all remaining ingredients except seafood and chili sauce. Blend.
3. Shape into oval or square on flat serving plate and cover with plastic wrap. Refrigerate overnight.
4. Right before serving, cover spread with chili sauce, then place shredded drained crabmeat or whole shrimps on top of chili sauce so that entire mold is covered.

Lox Spread

½ pound Lox
  (smoked salmon)
½ cup chopped onion
¾ cup tart apple
15 onion crackers

2 tablespoons white vinegar
3 tablespoons sugar
2 hard cooked eggs
  coarsely chopped

1. Peel apples; core and chop coarsely. Break crackers in small pieces and soak in vinegar 10 minutes.
2. Chop together all ingredients except egg, until very fine.
3. Add eggs.

Serve with onion crackers.

*(See page 26)

Shrimp Mold

2-5 ounce cans shrimp, drained
8 ounce package cream cheese
1 garlic bud, grated or pressed
   through garlic press

½ teaspoon Worcestershire sauce
1 teaspoon lemon juice
1 tablespoon mayonnaise

1. Grease mold with oil and drain.
2. Mix all ingredients together.
3. Chill over night in mold.

This recipe can be doubled and placed in a fish mold.

Shrimp Spread

1-8 ounce package frozen
   baby shrimp (cooked)
8 ounce package cream
   cheese
1 stick of margarine
1 can cream of shrimp soup

4 chopped green onions
Lemon juice
Worcestershire sauce
Garlic powder
Curry powder

1. Thaw and drain frozen shrimp (be certain all excess moisture is absorbed on paper toweling).
2. In mixing bowl beat cream cheese, margarine, and cream of shrimp soup.
3. Add seasoning to taste and green onions.
4. Fold in shrimp. Press into mold or form.

Make a day ahead. Serve with assorted crackers or melba toast.

Chipped Beef Spread

Serves 4 to 6

3 ounce package chipped
   beef
3 ounce package cream
   cheese
1 teaspoon chopped parsley
1 small sweet pickle chopped

1 tablespoon mayonnaise
Few drips onion juice
Dash garlic salt or powder
1 tablespoon Worcestershire
   sauce

1. Chop or dice beef and blend well with softened cream cheese, mayonnaise and seasonings.

Serve with party rye and assorted crackers.
May be thinned with sour cream to make an excellent dip.

Salmon-Avocado Spread

Makes 2 cups

1-7¾ ounce can red salmon
1 ripe avocado
1 tablespoon olive or salad oil

1 clove garlic, finely chopped
1½ teaspoons grated onion
½ teaspoon salt
4 drops of Tabasco

1. Drain and flake salmon.
2. Peel avocado, remove seed and mash.
3. Combine all ingredients and toss lightly.

Serve spread on crackers.

Salmon Mold

Serves 8-10

½ pound canned salmon
8 ounces cream cheese
½ teaspoon horseradish
2 teaspoons grated onion

¼ teaspoon salt
½ teaspoon liquid smoke
1 tablespoon lemon juice
¼ cup chopped parsley
1 cup chopped pecans

1. Drain salmon, remove skin and flake.
2. Mix all ingredients except parsley and pecans; shape in ball.
3. Roll in chopped parsley and chopped pecans.

Serve with crackers or party rye.

Tuna Paté

Makes 3 cups

1-8 ounce package cream
   cheese
2 tablespoons chili sauce
2 tablespoons snipped parsley

1 teaspoon instant minced
   onion
½ teaspoon hot pepper
   sauce (Tabasco)
2 (6½ or 7 ounce) cans tuna,
   drained

1. Blend softened cream cheese, chili sauce, parsley, onion and hot pepper sauce; gradually stir in drained tuna. Beat until mixture is thoroughly blended.
2. Pack in a 4 cup mold or small bowl.
3. Chill thoroughly, at least 3 hours or overnight.

At serving time, unmold on serving plate. If desired, garnish with sliced green olives. Serve with assorted crackers.

Mustard Sardine Spread

Serves 8

3 hard boiled eggs
Small or ½ grated onion
1 tablespoon mayonnaise

1 can mustard sardines, drained
1 teaspoon vinegar
Prepared mustard and pepper
to taste

1. Mash sardines and egg.
2. Add remaining ingredients.
3. Refrigerate a few hours.

Serve with party rye bread or crackers.
Does not taste like sardines. It is always fun to have your guests guess.

Sardine Spread

3 cans sardines packed in oil
2 hard boiled eggs
¼ to ½ cup applesauce

½ tablespoon minced onion
1 to 2 tablespoons mayonnaise

Bone and drain sardines, mash with remaining ingredients.

Anchovy Spread

8 ounce package cream
cheese
2 tablespoons milk

1 can flat anchovies
1 very small onion grated

1. Soften cream cheese with milk.
2. Add drained chopped anchovies and grated onion; mix well.

Serve with melba toast.

Pickled Shad Roe Spread

1 can shad roe
Juice of one lemon
2 tablespoons olive oil
Celery salt

Ground black pepper
Onion Salt
Garlic salt

1. Devein and remove all skin from shad roe (save juice). Crumble
   roe with fingers so that all eggs are separated.
2. Add juice from can and remaining ingredients, adding seasoning
   to taste.
3. Chill for several hours.

Some say this is better than caviar.

Mock Boursin au Poivre

8 ouncés cream cheese
1 clove garlic, crushed
1 teaspoon caraway seed
1 teaspoon basil

1 teaspoon dill weed
1 teaspoon chopped chives,
  dehydrated
Lemon pepper

1. Blend cream cheese with garlic, caraway, basil, dill weed and chives.
2. Pat into round flat shape.
3. Roll generously on all sides in lemon pepper.

Note: Make a few days ahead. Serve with assorted crackers. Tastes like French Boursin au Poivre. This spread gets instant raves.

Liptauer Cheese

1-3 oz. glass Old English cheese
  spread
1-3 oz. package cream cheese

3 tablespoons chili sauce
1 teaspoon paprika

Blend all ingredients until well mixed.

Appetizer Cheesecake

Don't let the title fool you—it isn't cake and there's no real cheese—but the flavor is delicious! Can be made a day ahead.

Serves 6 to 8

1 cup sour cream
¼ cup finely chopped green pepper
¼ cup finely chopped celery
2 tablespoons chopped pimiento
  stuffed olives
2 tablespoons chopped
  onion

1 teaspoon lemon juice
½ teaspoon Worcestershire sauce
Dash paprika
2 to 3 drops hot pepper sauce
2/3 cup cheese cracker crumbs
  (approximately 16 crackers)

1. Combine all ingredients except cracker crumbs.
2. Line 2½ cup bowl with plastic wrap.
3. Spread ½ cup sour cream mixture in bowl.
4. Reserve ¼ cup cracker crumbs for garnish.
5. Add layer of ½ of remaining crumbs.
6. Repeat layers of sour cream mixture and cracker crumbs.
7. Chill overnight.
8. Turn out on serving plate, remove plastic wrap and top with reserved crumbs.

Note: For a more pungemt flavor, mix 2-4 ounces of Roquefort, Bleu or Gorgonzola with sour cream at step 3. Serve with assorted crackers and vegetables.

Gorgonzola Cheese Spread

¾ pound butter
¾ pound Gorgonzola
1 teaspoon onion salt

⅛ teaspoon paprika
½ teaspoon MSG

1. Soften butter and cheese. Blend all ingredients.
2. Put in serving dish or shape into log.

An interesting spread made of a seldom used cheese.

Camembert Spread

1. Chill equal amounts of Camembert and butter; cut them into small pieces and combine them.
2. Add finely chopped onion to taste and a generous sprinkling of paprika.
3. Mix the ingredients until they hold together. (The texture should be chunky.)
4. Shape the mixture into a mound on a serving dish.

Sherry Cheese Paté

Serves 12

2-3 ounce packages
  cream cheese
4 ounces sharp Cheddar
  cheese, grated
2 tablespoons dry Sherry
½ teaspoon curry powder

¼ teaspoon salt
1-8 ounce jar chutney
2 green onions and tops

1. Chop chutney coarsely in blender; reserve.
2. Mix cheese, wine and seasonings throughly.
3. Put on pie plate and chill.
4. Spread chutney over top of cheese and sprinkle with finely chopped green onions.

An interesting combination of flavors.

Bleu Cheese-Caviar Spread

Serves 12

2-8 ounce packages cream cheese
4 ounces Bleu cheese or Roquefort
onion powder, to taste
3 or 4 tablespoons milk to soften

2 tablespoons lemon juice
1 tablespoon caraway seed
Small jar caviar

1. Blend all ingredients, except caviar.
2. Form into mound; make indentation in center and fill with caviar.

Watercress Spread

1 bunch watercress
1-8 ounce package cream cheese
1-3 ounce package cream cheese

1½ teaspoons horseradish
Dash of Worcestershire sauce

1. Finely chop watercress leaves.
2. Soften cream cheese. Mix all ingredients together.
3. Form into round ball.

Garnish with sprigs of parsley. Serve with miniature caraway rye.

Low Calorie Cheese Spread

Serves 6 or more

8 ounces Neufchatel cheese (low calorie)
2-3 tablespoons Worcestershire sauce

1. Place cheese in serving dish. Allow cheese to soften 4-5 hours.
2. Pour Worcestershire sauce over cheese.

A very easy, tasty low calorie spread, it is originally from New Orleans.

Note: Serve surrounded by carrot strips for dipping or as a spread with crackers.

Cheese in a Crock

2 cups assorted leftover
  cheeses
2 tablespoons cream cheese
2 tablespoons butter
2 tablespoons Scotch whiskey

4 tablespoons olive
  butter or chopped
  green olives
1 tablespoon caraway seed
Dash of cayenne
2 tablespoons olive oil

1. Grate enough cheese to make 2 cups. Combine with remaining ingredients and stir until smooth.
2. Pack into crock. Leave in refrigerator for 2 days or more before serving. This spread keeps for weeks and improves with aging.
3. Allow cheese to set out of refrigerator 1 hour before serving. Serve in crock, surrounded by green grapes and assorted crackers.

This is a great way to use up odds and ends of cheeses.

Replenish crock with more cheese and seasonings as needed.

Ingwiller Fromage

Serves 10-12
Makes 1½ cups

8 ounces cream cheese
  (room temperature)
½ green pepper, minced
1 small onion, minced
1 clove garlic, minced
1 tablespoon olive oil

2 tablespoons caraway seed
2 tablespoons red paprika
¼ teaspoon dry mustard
1-2 ounce can anchovies, undrained
Sour or sweet cream
  (to thin to spreading consistency)

1. Mix all ingredients until thoroughly blended.
2. Store in crock(s) in refrigerator till ready to serve.

Note: Can be made ahead and refrigerated indefinitely. This is a soft, creamy spread for crackers.

Chablis Spread

Makes 3/4 cup

1-3 ounce package cream cheese
1 clove garlic, crushed

2 ounces Liederkranz cheese
1 tablespoon Chablis wine

1. Work together all ingredients until smooth.
2. Cover tightly and refrigerate for 2 days.

Egg Salad Mold

Serves 24

18 hard boiled eggs
½ cup chopped green pepper
¼ cup diced pimiento
1/3 cup finely cut celery
3 tablespoons chili sauce
2 tablespoons chopped
   parsley

1 medium onion
   minced fine
2-8 ounce packages cream
   cheese
½ cup mayonnaise
Salt and pepper to taste

1. Shell eggs and mash.
2. Add green pepper, pimiento, celery, parsley, onion.
3.-Mash cheese, stir in mayonnaise, and chili sauce.
4. Combine with vegetables and cooled mashed eggs. Season well with salt and pepper.
5. Shape into a ring mold and chill it for four hours.

Loosen around the edge with a spatula and turn it out upside down on a chop plate. Fill the center with cherry tomatoes. Surround with crackers or party rye bread slices.

Chopped Egg and Onions

2 onions
8 hard cooked eggs
1½ teaspoons salt

¼ teaspoon freshly ground
   black pepper
4 tablespoons
   chicken fat (p. 108)

1. Chop the onions very fine.
2. Add the eggs and continue chopping.
3. Add the salt, pepper, and chicken fat. Mix lightly.
4. Correct seasoning.

Note: To serve, unmold. Spread with sour cream and garnish with red or black caviar.

Egg & Caviar Mold

12 hard boiled eggs
1 tablespoon raw onion, grated
2-4 tablespoons mayonnaise

Salt and pepper
Sour cream
Caviar

1. Chop eggs; add onion, salt and pepper to taste and sufficient mayonnaise to hold together.
2. Pack into greased mold. Chill several hours or overnight.

Note: To serve, unmold. Ice with sour cream and garnish with red or black caviar.

EASY WHEN YOU HAVE THE DOUGH

3

CONVENIENCE FOODS

Do rolling pins and floured boards strike terror to your heart? If kneading dough and sticky fingers are not your bag, you still can dazzle your guests with marvelous little flaky treats, thanks to today's convenience foods. Straight from your supermarket shelves, these prepared doughs are easy to handle, and take just minutes to fill and bake with whatever choice morsels you desire.

Sardines in Blankets

8 canapes

1-4 ounce can small sardines in mustard sauce
1-8 ounce can crescent dinner rolls

1. Drain sardines on paper towels; reserve mustard sauce.
2. Unroll roll of dough. Break apart on perforations into 8 triangles.
3. Brush each triangle with mustard sauce.
4. Place a sardine on wide end of triangle; roll up.
5. Place on greased baking sheet, seam side down.
6. Bake at 375° for 10-12 minutes or until dough is nicely browned.

Serve immediately or keep hot on electric tray.

Smoked Oyster En Croute

1 can smoked oysters
1 can Crescent rolls

1. Drain oysters.
2. Separate rolls. Cut into 1½" squares.
3. Place oyster in center of square. Wrap dough, sealing carefully.
4. Place on greased baking sheet.
5. Bake at 375° for 8-10 minutes or until dough is nicely browned.

The delicate smoky flavor of the smoked oyster and the crunchy texture of the flaky roll dough are a tasteful combination. Serve immediately or keep warm on electric tray.

Note: Keep roll dough <u>very</u> cold for ease in handling.

Easy Knishes

Serves 12 (about 36 pieces)

1 can refrigerated butterflake rolls
2 cups leftover meat (roast, steak, brisket, etc.)

1 onion
1 egg
Salt and pepper

1. Grind meat with raw onion and mix in egg and salt and pepper.
2. Separate layers of dough from rolls into small rounds (they will already be buttered).
3. Place about ¼ teaspoon of meat mixture on each dough round and pinch closed.
4. Bake at 350° on cookie sheet until light brown (about 8 to 10 minutes). Serve hot.

Can be frozen on cookie sheet (before baking) and then bagged to store in freezer. To serve, thaw and then bake as above. Keep hot on electric tray.

Note: Keep roll dough very cold for ease in handling.

Miniature Meat Turnovers

Makes 32 turnovers

1 envelope Lipton Beef Flavor Mushroom Mix
½ pound ground beef
1 cup drained bean sprouts

½ cup sliced water chestnuts
2 tablespoons chopped onion
2 packages refrigerator crescent rolls

1. Preheat oven 375°F.
2. In medium skillet, combine first five ingredients; brown well.
3. Separate crescent dough as package directs; cut in half. Place spoonful of mixture in center of each triangle; fold over and seal edges.
4. Place on ungreased cookie sheet; bake 15 minutes or until golden.

This recipe is one of Lipton's own perennial favorites, good in taste and texture.

Arnipita
(Greek Lamb Pastries)

Makes 8 rolls or 32 pieces

1 pound lean ground lamb	2 eggs
½ pound lean ground beef	½ teaspoon seasoned salt
2 tablespoons tomato paste	Olive oil
2 tablespoons dehydrated onions	8 sheets Phyllo pastry (12x16)
½ cup pistachio nuts or pine nuts	

1. Saute ground meats, mixing with a fork until browned and well separated.
2. Drain excess fat.
3. Add tomato paste, seasoned salt, onions and chopped nuts.
4. Cool a few minutes and stir in beaten eggs.
5. Thaw Phyllo pastry according to directions on package. Unroll and remove one sheet of pastry.
6. Lay the sheet of pastry on a tea towel. Brush half with olive oil, as in diagram A. Fold on line shown. (You will now have an 8" by 12" rectangle.)
7. Brush surface with olive oil. Spread 1/3 cup filling on area shown in diagram B.
8. Fold in long sides 1½" on dotted lines of diagram B to hold filling inside of roll.
9. Form into roll by raising towel at filled end of pastry. This will start it forming into a tight roll.
10. Place on greased pan, seam side down. Brush with a little olive oil.
11. Bake at 400° for 15-18 minutes or until browned. Drain on wire rack for 5 minutes. Serve warm. Slice into 4 pieces.

May be made ahead through step 10, covered, and refrigerated until ready to bake or baked, frozen and reheated at 350 till well warmed. Keep hot on electric tray.

Delicious, crisp and spicy—a delicate crust.

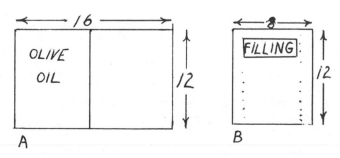

51

Hamburger Pinwheels

Serves 8

1 small onion minced
1 pound ground beef
1 teaspoon salt

⅛ teaspoon pepper
¼ teaspoon Worcestershire sauce
1 package refrigerator biscuits

1. Cook onion in small amount of fat until tender but not brown. Add meat and cook until browned. Drain off fat.
2. Season with salt, pepper and Worcestershire sauce.
3. Roll out biscuit dough into a rectangle ¼ inch thick. Spread meat on dough and roll like a jelly roll.
4. Cut into slices about 1½ inches thick. Place cut side up on greased baking sheet and bake in hot oven (400° F.) about 15 minutes.

Mimi's Pizza

3 boxes of English muffins
2 small cans of tomato sauce
1-8 oz. package of Mozzarella cheese

2 sticks of pepperoni
Parmesan cheese
Oregano

1. Slice muffins in half.
2. Spread each piece with tomato sauce.
3. Sprinkle with oregano and Parmesan cheese.
4. Put four thin slices of pepperoni on each half and cut the halves in half again if smaller servings are wanted.
5. Put thin slices of Mozzarella cheese on top.
6. Place on cookie sheet.
7. Bake in a very hot oven until cheese bubbles, which takes about 10 minutes.

Blintz Soufflé

Serves 6

½ stick butter or margarine
3 eggs
1 cup sour cream

Pinch of salt
1 package frozen
  cheese blintzes

1. Melt butter (or margarine) in casserole. Place six frozen blintzes in casserole.
2. Blend remaining ingredients and pour over blintzes.
3. Bake 1 hour at 350°.

Pizza

1-15 ounce can Hunt's tomato sauce
 with tomato bits
1-8 ounce package Mozzarella
 cheese
⅛ teaspoon oregano
1-4 ounce can sliced mushrooms,
 drained

1 pound bacon, chopped, fried
 and drained
1 tablespoon olive oil
Salt, pepper, Accent
2 tablespoons grated Parmesan
½ loaf frozen bread dough

1. Thaw loaf of frozen bread dough. Roll ½ loaf into thin circle to fit 15" pizza pan.
2. Grease pan. Place circle of dough into pan. Brush dough with oil.
3. Spread cheese over dough. Pour tomato sauce on cheese. Sprinkle with seasonings.
4. Spread mushrooms and bacon over pizza*. Sprinkle with 1 tablespoon olive oil and then Parmesan.
5. Bake on lowest shelf of oven at 425° for 20 minutes or until crust is browned on bottom.

Cut into squares for hors d'oeuvre. Keep hot on electric tray. This pizza may be baked, cooled completely, wrapped airtight and frozen for future use. Bake at 400° to thaw pizza and crispen crust.

* Olives, green peppers, sausage, meatballs may be used in addition to or instead of bacon and mushrooms.

Pigs in Blankets

Thaw frozen bread dough according to directions on package. Drain Vienna sausage or cocktail weiners on paper towels. Slice in half. Wrap a small amount of dough around to cover completely. Refrigerate until one hour before serving. Let rise in warm place for 45 minutes. Bake at 350° until browned, about 10-15 minutes.

Cheese and Artichoke Appetizers

4 baked patty shells
2-3 ounce packages cream
   cheese with chives
3 drops Tabasco sauce

2 tablespoons soft butter
1 egg
6 drops Worcestershire sauce
4 canned artichoke hearts (drained)

1. Place patty shells on a fire-proof serving dish.
2. Beat cheese with butter, egg and seasoning.
3. Place spoonful of cheese mixture in bottom of each patty shell, set an artichoke heart in the center and cover with remaining cheese.
4. Bake for about 30 minutes in the upper third of a pre-heated 475° oven until the cheese filling has puffed slightly and browned on top.

Note: An elegant first course for a dinner party; also nice when friends stop in for cocktails.

Mushroom and Cream Cheese Logs

Makes 16 pieces

3 ounces chopped mushrooms
¼ teaspoon seasoned salt
1-8 ounce package refrigerator
   crescent rolls

1-3 ounce package cream cheese
1 beaten egg

1. Mince mushrooms. Blend well with softened cream cheese and salt.
2. Divide filling among the four rectangles of the crescent roll package and spread to cover.
3. Roll up, starting at long sides. Cut in 1½″ pieces.
4. Brush with beaten egg and sprinkle with poppy seeds (optional).
5. Bake on ungreased baking sheet in 375° oven for about 12 minutes. Remove to rack.

Can be prepared a few hours ahead and left refrigerated until time to bake. Keep hot on electric tray.

Note: Canned mushrooms are good; but sautéed fresh mushrooms are even better.

HOT
PICKUPS

4

Pirogen

Pastry

1½ cups sifted flour
½ teaspoon salt
½ teaspoon baking powder

½ cup shortening
1 egg beaten
2 tablespoons cold water

1. Sift the flour, salt, and baking powder into a bowl.
2. Cut in the shortening with a pastry blender or 2 knives.
3. Add the egg and cold water, tossing lightly until a ball of dough is formed.
4. Chill while preparing the filling.

Mushroom Filling for Pirogen

3 Tbsp. shortening
1 lb. mushrooms, chopped
2 onions, chopped
2 Tbsp. chopped parsley
1 Tbsp. chopped dill (optional)

2 hard cooked egg yolks, mashed
1½ tsp. salt
¼ tsp. freshly ground black pepper
½ cup bread crumbs
2 Tbsp. sour cream (optional)

1. Melt the shortening in a skillet.
2. Add the mushrooms and onions. Sauté for 10 minutes, or until the mushroom liquid is evaporated.
3. Add the parsley, dill, egg yolks, salt, pepper, bread crumbs, and sour cream. Mix well.
4. Preheat oven to 375°.
5. Roll the dough ⅛ inch thick on a lightly floured surface.
6. Cut into 3 inch circles.
7. Place a tablespoon of mushroom filling on each. Fold the dough over the filling, sealing the edges well.
8. Place on a greased baking sheet. Bake for 20 minutes, or until browned.

Miniature Reuben

1 package small party rye bread
Corned beef
Russian dressing

Sauerkraut, well drained
Slices processed Swiss cheese
(each cut in 4 squares)

1. Spread a little Russian dressing on one side rye bread slice.
2. Place a piece of corned beef on bread. Place a small amount of sauerkraut on corned beef and top with ¼ square of cheese.
3. Bake in 350° oven until cheese melts.

Dora Ang's Fried Wontons

Wonton Wrapper

10-15 wontons

1 cup flour   ½ teaspoon salt
1 egg   1/3 cup water

1. Mix ingredients in a bowl and knead until very smooth, about 5 minutes.
2. Cover with a damp cloth and let rest 15-30 minutes.
3. Remove a portion of the dough to a board lightly sprinkled with cornstarch.
4. Roll dough, turning frequently until very thin.
5. Cut into 3-4 inch squares.
6. Continue until all dough is used.

Freeze if not using right away. Thaw one hour before using.

Wonton Filling

8 ounces ground pork   1 teaspoon salt
   or beef   Dash of pepper
1 egg   ½ teaspoon sesame oil
2 tablespoons chopped green   Vegetable oil
   onion (including green tops)
1 tablespoon soy sauce

1. If using pork, brown first in skillet. Drain.
2. Place meat in a bowl and add egg, onions, salt, soy sauce and pepper. Mix well.
3. Let stand for 20 to 30 minutes.
4. Add sesame oil. It is important to add this ingredient only just before filling wrappers.
5. Place about 1 teaspoon filling in center of each square of wrapper. Fold corner to corner to make a triangle. Pinch together the widest two outer corners, so that the filled wonton folds up. Moisten edges with water to seal.
6. Heat vegetable oil in a pan to 350° and fry wontons until golden brown, about 2 minutes.

Serve hot with ginger sauce for dipping. These filled wontons can be frozen after frying. To reheat for serving, preheat oven to 400°. Turn down to 300° and heat frozen wontons for 5 minutes or until heated through.

GINGER SAUCE FOR WONTONS

1 tablespoon sugar
1 tablespoon white vinegar
Dash of salt
1/3 cup water

1 tablespoon tomato catsup
1 teaspoon cornstarch
1 teaspoon freshly
  chopped ginger root

1. Boil water.
2. Add sugar, salt, catsup and vinegar. Remove from heat.
3. Stir in cornstarch and add ginger.

This sauce can be served warm or cooled. It may be made ahead and refrigerated. This will give it a spicier taste.

The Wonton wrappers may be purchased frozen.

Foo Young Fritters

Makes about 48

6 eggs
1 cup self-rising flour
1 can bean sprouts,
  well-drained
1 cup cooked chicken, chopped
  (or tuna fish)

1 tablespoon soy sauce
½ teaspoon Worcestershire sauce
1 envelope onion soup mix
1-4 ounce can mushroom
  pieces, drained
1 can water chestnuts
  (sliced)

1. Beat eggs slightly.
2. Blend in flour, soy sauce, Worcestershire sauce till smooth. Stir in remaining ingredients.
3. Drop by teaspoonsful into hot oil. Fry at 350° for a few minutes till golden brown.
4. Drain on paper towel.

Note: An Oriental dish with a Southern Flavor, y'all.
Can be frozen and reheated for serving.

Fish Patties

1-6 ounce can tuna, salmon,
  drained or any leftover fish
1 large cooked & mashed potato
1 small onion, fried and cut fine bits

1 egg
Salt and pepper, to taste
Dash of catsup
Bread crumbs

1. Mix all ingredients together.
2. Form into small patties, (size of a quarter). Dip in bread crumbs.
3. Fry to a light brown color.

Note: Serve patties dry or with a can of undiluted mushroom soup, or a sauce.

Party Turnovers

PASTRY
1/3 cup shortening (half butter,
    half vegetable shortening
¾ cup flour
Pinch salt
2-3 tablespoons cold water

FILLINGS
1 cup ground salami and
    ½ teaspoon horseradish
        or
1 cup ground chicken
¼ teaspoon curry powder
¼ teaspoon salt
3 tablespoons minced
    fresh parsley
    or 1 tablespoon dehydrated
    parsley

1. Make pastry by cutting in together the shortening, flour and salt. Add water, 1 tablespoon at a time, using only enough to make dough hold together. Form into ball. Chill ½ hour.
2. Roll pastry ⅛" thick. Cut into 2 " squares.
3. Put 1 teaspoon of filling mixture in center of square. Fold into a triangle. Press edges together with fork.

When ready to serve, fry in hot fat (320°) for four minutes. Drain on paper towel.

Serve immediately or keep hot on electric hot tray.

Hot Potato

Serves 6

4 strips of crisp crumbled bacon
1 stick (¼ lb.) of butter
1 clove of minced garlic
1 tablespoon of chopped parsley

18 small unpeeled
    new potatoes
Salt and pepper to taste

1. Cream butter. Then add rest of ingredients.
2. Potatoes may be baked (greased and pierced first) if desired or boiled.

Serve potatoes and sauce in separate bowls; sauce should be at room temperature. Make sauce ahead and refrigerate.

Men love it. Fattening but good!

This is a good sauce for potatoes served for a buffet supper.

Breaded Artichoke Hearts (Italian Style)

2 cans artichoke hearts
8 ounce bottle Italian dressing
¼ cup grated Romano cheese

1½ cup Italian-
flavored bread crumbs

1. Drain artichoke hearts and slice into halves or quarters.
2. Marinate in Italian dressing for 8 hours, then drain.
3. Place bread crumbs and cheese in a bag. Add artichoke hearts and shake in bag until well coated.
4. Spread on baking sheet and bake 12 to 15 minutes at 375°.

Note: A delectable Roman valentine, if you have the heart!

Artichoke Bubbles

16 slices small party rye bread
1 can (14 ounce) artichoke
   hearts, drained
1 egg white
2 tablespoons grated Parmesan cheese

1 tablespoon mayonnaise
1 tablespoon shredded Cheddar
   cheese
Dash cayenne pepper

1. Place bread slices on baking sheet. Cut artichoke hearts in half; place one half, cut side down, on each slice of bread.
2. Beat egg white until stiff. Fold in remaining ingredients. Spread on bread. Sprinkle with paprika.
3. Top each heart with one half teaspoon of eggwhite mixture. Sprinkle with paprika.
4. Bake 10-15 minutes until golden brown at 400°.

Stuffed Artichoke Bottoms

1 package frozen
  artichoke bottoms (20)
1 small can chopped black olives

¼ cup grated onion
¾ cup grated Cheddar cheese
4 tablespoons mayonnaise

1. Cook artichoke bottoms according to directions on package. Drain.
2. Combine remaining ingredients and stuff package cavity of artichokes.
3. Preheat oven to 350. Place artichokes on cookie sheet and bake 10 minutes or until cheese is bubbling.

Note: As a variation, use this stuffing for raw mushrooms and broil 3-5 minutes.

Canned artichoke bottoms may be substituted. May be prepared through step 2 and baked when ready to serve.

Artichoke-Clam Puffs

Makes about 36 pieces

2 pkgs. frozen artichoke hearts
¼ teaspoon hot pepper sauce
1-6½ oz. can minced clams, drained
Paprika

1-8 oz. pkg. cream cheese
2 tablespoons Sherry

1. Cook artichokes according to package directions (do not overcook). Drain.
2. Beat cream cheese with pepper sauce and sherry, then stir in clams.
3. Spoon mixture onto cut side of the artichokes and sprinkle with paprika.
4. Broil until browned.

Canned artichoke bottoms may be substituted.

Stuffed Curried Eggs

Serves 4

6 hard boiled eggs
Mayonnaise
Curry powder, to taste
2 tablespoons butter

2 tablespoons flour
1 cup milk
½ teaspoon Worcestershire sauce
Salt and pepper, to taste

1. Peel eggs and remove yolks. Mash yolks with enough mayonnaise and curry powder to make a good consistency.
2. Stuff yolk mixture back into whites. Put them in a shallow casserole.
3. Make a cream sauce from remaining ingredients.
4. Pour over eggs and bake at 350° for 15 minutes.

Hot Asparagus Canapé

For each canapé:
1 thin frozen slice white bread
1 thin slice Prosciutto

1 stalk canned asparagus,
  drained
Butter
Parmesan cheese

1. Remove crusts from white bread. Roll each slice flat between two sheets of waxed paper.
2. Spread frozen bread with softened butter. Sprinkle with Parmesan.
3. Thaw bread; place 1 slice Prosciutto and 1 stalk of asparagus on corner of bread. Roll and fasten with toothpick. Brush with melted butter. Sprinkle with Parmesan.
4. Bake 10-12 minutes at 400°.

Do ahead and freeze; keeps for months if well wrapped. These can be prepared through Step 3, and refrigerated or frozen until baking.

Toasted Mushroom Rolls
Makes 3½ dozen canapés

½ pound mushrooms,
  finely chopped
3 tablespoons flour
¼ teaspoon MSG
2 teaspoons minced chives
1 large loaf sliced fresh white bread
  (20 or 24 oz. size)

¼ cup butter or margarine
¾ teaspoon salt
1 cup light cream or milk
1 teaspoon lemon juice

1. Sauté mushrooms in shortening.
2. Blend in flour, salt and MSG.
3. Stir in cream or milk. Cook until thick.
4. Add chives, lemon juice. Cool.
5. Remove crusts from slices of bread. Roll thin.
6. Spread with mixture. Roll up.
7. Pack and freeze if desired.
8. To serve, defrost, cut each roll in half and toast on all sides in 400° oven.

Note: For a more elegant and expensive dish, add 1 lb. lobster meat, minced, to the mushroom mixture. Follow directions for bread using 2 regular loaves. Proceed as above. Makes about 6 dozen luscious canapés.

Refrigerator Cheese Rolls

Makes 3 dozen canapes

½ pound aged Cheddar cheese
1 tablespoon soft butter
½ teaspoon garlic salt

3 tablespoons mayonnaise
2 teaspoons Worcestershire Sauce
1 16-ounce loaf white
   bread, sliced

1. Grate cheese, add next four ingredients.
2. Remove crusts from slices of white bread. Roll thin.
3. Spread cheese mixture on bread and roll up.
4. Refrigerate or freeze.
5. To serve, return to room temperature and slice each roll in half. Broil until lightly browned.

Crispy Cheese Rolls

Makes about 4 doz. canapes

½ pound crock sharp cheese
½ pound Meunster cheese
¼ pound Bleu cheese
1 tablespoon butter

2 eggs
1-1 pound loaf of sliced
   bread
½ pound melted butter
½ pound chopped nuts

1. Blend Bleu cheese, sharp cheese and butter in an electric mixer. Add softened Meunster and beat until smooth. Add eggs and beat until mixture is well blended.
2. Cut crusts off bread slices. Roll out very thin with rolling pin.
3. Spread with cheese and roll up like a jelly roll. Cut each roll in half.
4. Brush with melted butter. Roll in nuts.
5. Place on baking sheet, seam side down.
6. Bake 5 minutes at 450°.

These tangy crisp canapes can be prepared through step 5 in advance and frozen for future use. When frozen solid remove from baking sheet, place in airtight plastic bags and return to freezer. Remove and bake in small quantities as needed.

"Emergency" Canapé

Ritz crackers
Velveeta cheese
Catsup or chili sauce

1. Place a small square of cheese on cracker with a dot of catsup or chili sauce in middle.
2. Broil until cheese melts a bit.

Great for unexpected guests.

Corned Beef Hash Canapé

1 can corned beef hash
1 small jar pickle slices
Durkee's dressing

Bread (preferably thin) with
crusts removed

1. Cut bread in rounds with small glass or cookie cutter.
2. Spread on Durkee's dressing.
3. Press down a pickle slice on top.
4. Make a meat ball of rounded teaspoon of hash.
5. Press meatball on top of pickle.
6. Broil at about 350° until meat is well heated (about 8 minutes).
   Broil 3 inches from heat so that bread will not burn.

These can be made ahead and frozen.

Deviled Ham Puffs

Serves 8

½ pound cream cheese
½ teaspoon baking powder
1 teaspoon milk
1 egg yolk

2-2¼ ounce cans deviled ham
30 to 35 small rounds of
   white bread

1. Blend cheese, baking powder, milk and egg yolk together.
2. Toast bread on one side.
3. Spread untoasted side with deviled ham, cover with a mound of
   cheese mixture.
4. Bake at 375° for 10 to 12 minutes or until puffed and slightly
   browned.

Make ahead and bake when ready to serve.

Ham & Chutney Canapés

¼ pound ham
4 tablespoons chutney
2 tablespoons chili sauce

2 teaspoons horseradish
Toast rounds
Sliced sharp Cheddar

1. Grind ham. Mix with chutney, chili sauce and horseradish.
2. Toast small rounds of bread.
3. Just before serving, spread toast rounds with ham mixture. Dot
   with cheese.
4. Put under broiler or bake at 475° till cheese melts.

Tuna Canapés

Makes 3 dozen canapés

3 dozen bread rounds,
 1½ to 1¾″ diameter
1-7 oz. can tuna, drained
2 tablespoons finely
 chopped onion
2 tablespoons chopped green
 pepper
1 tablespoon chopped pimiento
¼ cup mayonnaise

¼ cup sour cream
1 teaspoon Worcestershire
2 teaspoons lemon juice
Dash of pepper
¼ cup packaged grated
 American cheese product
2 egg whites,
 stiffly beaten

1. Place bread rounds on a cookie sheet and broil until lightly browned on one side.
2. Combine tuna, onion, green pepper, pimiento, mayonnaise, sour cream, Worcestershire, lemon juice, pepper and grated cheese. Blend.
3. Fold in stiffly beaten egg whites.
4. Top untoasted side of bread rounds with a mound of the mixture.
5. Broil about 4″ from heat until puffed and browned. Serve immediately.

This recipe may be prepared in advance through step 2. Just before serving, continue at step 3.

Clam Puffs

Makes 24 toast rounds

7 ounce can minced clams
2 tablespoons heavy cream
1-3 ounce pkg. cream cheese
¼ teaspoon dry mustard
½ teaspoon Worcestershire sauce

¼ teaspoon salt
1 teaspoon finely minced onion
24 toast rounds
Paprika

1. Drain clams.
2. Combine all ingredients except paprika.
3. Spread on toast rounds.
4. Place under broiler until puffy.
5. Sprinkle with paprika; serve hot.

Note: Spread can be made ahead and refrigerated. Spread on toast before ready to serve.

Italian Rye Chips

½ pound grated Swiss cheese
2 tablespoons mayonnaise
Pinah rye chips

Small onion grated or
onion salt to taste

1. Mix cheese, mayonnaise and onion.
2. Put 1 teaspoon on top of each cracker.
3. Broil until brown and bubbly.

*Note: Can be made ahead and refrigerated. Broil when ready to serve.
Pinah rye chips are available at specialty food shops...and are worth
the search.*

Cheese Canapés

Makes about 2 dozen small canapés

8 ounces port wine-flavored
Cheddar cheese
1/3 cup chopped ripe olives

1/3 cup mayonnaise
½ teaspoon dry mustard
Freshly ground black pepper

1. Combine all ingredients.
2. Spread on Melba toast rounds or party rye bread and heat in hot
   oven (450°) for about 5 minutes.

> Here is the traditional cheese puff - with a difference. Other
> cheeses...other flavors. Give these variations a try.

Cheese Puffs

1 loaf unsliced white bread
½ pound sharp Cheddar cheese
4 egg whites, stiffly beaten

6 ounce cream cheese
2 sticks butter

1. Melt cheeses and butter in double boiler.
2. When cool fold in stiffly beaten egg whites.
3. Cut crust off bread, and cut bread in 1" cubes, dip in cheese mixture; place on cookie sheet and refrigerate overnight.
4. Bake at 400° for 10 to 12 minutes. Serve warm.
Note: Can be frozen.

Swiss Sandwich Puffs

Makes 32 puffs

½ cup mayonnaise
2 tablespoons snipped parsley
8 slices Swiss cheese

¼ cup chopped onion
32 tiny rye slices

1. Combine mayonnaise, onion and parsley.
2. Spread on very lightly toasted rye slices.
3. Top each slice with ¼ of a slice of Swiss cheese.
4. Broil 2-3 minutes.

Roquefort Puffs

Makes 8 canapes

1 egg white
2 ounces Roquefort cheese spread

8 crackers or 8—2 inch bread rounds
paprika

1. Beat egg white until stiff.
2. Mix cheese till creamy.
3. Fold in beaten egg white and heap on cracker or bread round.
4. Bake in slow oven 300° for 15 minutes or until brown. Garnish with paprika.

Toasted Cheese Rounds

½ cup mayonnaise
¼ cup Parmesan cheese, grated
Salt and pepper to taste

Very, very thin onion slices
Dash of Worcestershire sauce
1½" diameter bread circles
   (cut with a shot glass) or
   rye rounds

1. Mix mayonnaise with cheese and seasonings.
2. Put one slice of onion on each circle of bread.
3. Cover onion with mayonnaise mixture. Sprinkle with additional grated Parmesan.
4. Place under broiler until brown.

Note: Can be made ahead, covered, and refrigerated until ready to serve.

Toasted Cheese Appetizer

1 package shredded Cheddar cheese
1 package shredded Mozarella cheese
Grated Parmesan cheese to taste
Grated onion to taste, or onion powder
Mayonnaise

1. Mix all ingredients, adding enough mayonnaise to blend well.
2. Spread mixture on sesame rounds.
3. Place on cookie sheet and broil until cheese bubbles. This takes just a few minutes so watch them closely.

Easy and good for the "spur-of-the-moment" get-together. The sesame and cheese are a great combination.

CHEDDAR CHEESE PASTRY

Ha' Pennies

1 stick butter or margarine
½ pound grated sharp Cheddar
   cheese
½ package dry onion soup mix
1 cup flour

1. Soften shortening and cheese together at room temperature. Blend together.
2. Add onion soup mix and flour to form stiff dough.
3. Shape into rolls about 1" in diameter. Wrap in waxed paper and chill.
4. Cut into slices about ¼" thick.
5. Bake on ungreased baking sheet in 375° oven for 10 to 15 minutes. If desired, top with a pecan, almond or walnut before baking.
6. Remove from pan. Cool on wire rack. Store in airtight can.

A very tasty appetizer.

Cheddar Cheese Crisps

1 pound Cheddar cheese
3½ cups flour
1¾ sticks margarine, softened
2 drops Tabasco sauce
1 teaspoon Worcestershire

1. Grate cheese and mash well with the margarine. Add Tabasco and Worcestershire.
2. Stir in flour and mix well.
3. Shape into a 1" roll, put in foil and refrigerate several hours.
4. Remove from refrigerator, cut in ¼" slices, place on cookie sheets, bake 12 to 15 minutes in 350° oven until lightly browned.
5. Remove from pan. Cool on wire rack. Store in airtight can.

Can be made ahead of time, refrigerated or frozen until ready to bake.

Variations of Cheddar Cheese Pastry

(See Page 69)

Pecan Pastry
Add 1 cup chopped pecans for each cup of flour.

Onion Pastry
Add ½ package Lipton's onion soup mix for each cup of flour.

Marmalade Turnovers

Cut pastry into circles. Put ½ teaspoon of marmalade in center of circle, fold over edge and mash edges together with a fork. Bake 375 degrees for 10 minutes. Keep in covered tin. They freeze beautifully after being baked. Reheat thoroughly before serving. Makes 2 to 3 dozen.

Golden Olive Nuggets

Drain olives and pat dry. Use about 1 teaspoon dough for each olive, wrapping the olive with the dough. Roll in seeds of your choice. Bake 15 minutes in preheated 400° oven and serve while warm. Makes about 36 nuggets.

These may be frozen before baking and popped into the oven when ready to serve. Arrange on baking sheet and freeze firm. Store in plastic bag in freezer. To serve, thaw and bake as directed.

For an interesting variation, wrap cheese pastry around almond stuffed or onion stuffed olives. The canapes can be rolled in sesame seed before baking for added crunchiness and flavor.

Mushrooms Stuffed with Spinach

Serves 10

1 pound mushrooms
1-10 ounce pkg. frozen spinach
1 stick butter

1 tablespoon chopped onion
salt, pepper, nutmeg,
grated cheddar cheese

1. Wash and drain mushrooms. Remove stems and chop.
2. Sauté onion in ½ butter. Then sauté chopped mushroom stems.
3. Remove with slotted spoon. Add remaining butter and carefully sauté mushroom caps for a short time to coat them well with butter.
4. Cook and drain spinach. Put in blender with mushroom stems, onion and seasoning. Purée.
5. Fill mushroom caps with mixture. Sprinkle with grated cheese.
6. Bake at 375° for 15 minutes.

Note: If large mushroom caps are used they make a nice vegetable garnish for steak dinner.

Stuffed Mushrooms

Serves 6

24 large mushrooms
3 tablespoons low calorie cream
  cheese
1 tablespoon butter

3 green onions
Salt and pepper
1 tablespoon seasoned bread crumbs

1. Clean mushroom caps and dry.
2. Chop mushroom stems and sauté with cut-up green onions, salt, and pepper in butter.
3. Remove from heat and add crumbs and cream cheese to mushroom mixture.
4. Stuff mushroom caps and place in baking dish that has thin layer of milk in it so mushrooms will not stick.
5. Bake 15 minutes at 350°.

Make ahead and refrigerate until baking time.

Mushrooms-All Puffed Up

1 pound fresh mushrooms
¼ cup butter
¼ cup chopped onion
Bread rounds - 2" in diameter as many as there are mushrooms

Salt, pepper, pinch of sugar
1 cup crumbled Bleu cheese
2 eggs beaten

1. Clean mushrooms. Remove stems. Drain caps and stems.
2. Sauté mushroom caps in butter about two minutes. Set aside to cool.
3. Chop stems and sauté with onions in butter. Add seasonings. Mix well.
4. Spread chopped mixture on bread rounds.
5. Mix eggs and cheese. Form into balls to fit inside mushroom caps.
6. Fill caps with cheese balls. Put filled mushrooms on toast rounds.
7. Broil 3" 4" from heat 7 10 minutes or until cheese is lightly browned and puffy.

(Can be made ahead and broiled at the last minute.)

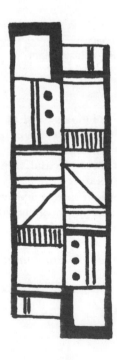

Nashville Nosh

Ground hot sausage meat
Mushrooms

1. Wash and dry mushrooms.
2. Take stems off mushrooms.
3. Fill with sausage.
4. Broil for 10 minutes.

Note: Keep hot on electric tray. Insist you've been working on these all day.

Simple Stuffed Mushrooms

24 large mushrooms
½ stick butter
Deviled ham or sharp cheese spread

1. Wash and dry 24 large mushrooms. Remove stems.
2. Melt butter in skillet. Add mushrooms in one layer. Turn when edges begin to brown. (Cooking should take 4 to 5 minutes).
3. Drain on paper toweling.
4. Fill with deviled ham or any sharp cheese spread.
5. Just before serving, heat for a few minutes in a 350° oven.

Note: Make ahead. Refrigerate until ready to use.

Meat Filled Mushroom Caps

Makes 2 dozen

24 large mushrooms
½ cup soy sauce
½ pound ground beef
¼ cup minced green pepper
2 tablespoons bread crumbs
1 egg yolk
1 tablespoon minced onion
½ clove minced garlic
¼ teaspoon salt
¼ teaspoon pepper

1. Wash and drain mushroom caps; remove stems.
2. Marinate caps for 1 hour in soy sauce.
3. Finely chop stems and mix with remaining ingredients.
4. Drain caps, reserve soy sauce. Stuff with meat mixture, mounded high. Brush tops with reserved soy sauce.
5. Broil 8-10 minutes.

May be served immediately after broiling. If you wish to "do it ahead", broil; refrigerate or freeze. When ready to serve, defrost and bake at 350° for 8-10 minutes.

Mushrooms Flambé

Serves 8-10

3 tablespoons butter
2 tablespoons oil
1 pound fresh mushrooms
Salt
Pepper
Tarragon

Chives
Parsley
4 tablespoons Sherry
1 tablespoon lemon juice
Few grains sugar
1 jigger brandy

1. Heat butter and oil in chafing dish. Sauté mushrooms.

2. Add herbs, spices, Sherry, and lemon juice. Cover and cook 3-4 minutes.
3. Add sugar, heated brandy and ignite.

Serve on toothpicks. This recipe is elegant and easy. Make it in your chafing dish.

Mushroom Puffs

Makes 35 to 40 puffs

1-4 ounce can button mushrooms
1-8 ounce package cream cheese, softened
½ small onion, minced
1 loaf of thinly sliced bread

Garlic powder
Lawry's seasoned salt
2 egg yolks
salt, pepper

1. Cut bread into rounds 1½" in diameter with cookie cutter or juice glass. Place a mushroom in center.
2. Mix cream cheese with egg yolks and onions. Add rest of seasoning to taste.
3. Cover mushroom with cheese mixture.
4. Place under broiler until brown and puffy.

Cheese and Mushroom Canapés

Makes 2½ dozen

¼ pound mushrooms
1 tablespoon butter
1-8 ounce package cream cheese
Cream

1 teaspoon minced onions
Salt and pepper
Small rounds of bread
Butter for rounds of toasted bread

1. Chop mushrooms in tiny pieces. Cook for a few minutes in butter.
2. Mix mushrooms with cream cheese, salt, pepper and minced onion and enough cream to soften.
3. Toast small rounds of bread on one side.
4. Spread untoasted side with butter, then mushroom mixture. Refrigerate or freeze.
5. When ready to serve, place under broiler until puffy and brown.

Cheese Puffs (Very Easy)
Will serve 10 (if other canapes will be served, too)

1 cup grated sharp cheese	1 tablespoon flour
1 teaspoon garlic salt	1 tablespoon dry sherry
Crustless bread cut into quarters	2 egg whites

1. Mix flour, seasoning and cheese; stir in wine.
2. Beat egg whites until stiff and fold into first mixture.
3. Drop by the level tablespoon onto a cookie sheet.
4. Freeze, then transfer frozen cheese "drops" to a plastic bag for longer freezer storage.
5. To serve: place a frozen cheese ball on ¼ slice square of crustless bread, or place a frozen cheese ball on crisp cracker.
6. Arrange on a cookie sheet and heat for about 5 minutes in a 350° oven or until cheese mixture begins to bubble.

Note: For microwave oven:
Place the frozen cheese balls on crackers or bread on a 7-inch round paper plate. Heat in microwave oven for 1¾ to 2 minutes before serving.

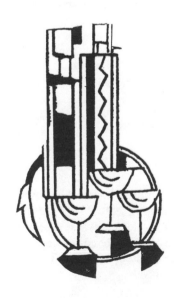

RUMAKI

Rumaki and Other Bacon Treats

General Instructions:
1. Cut bacon slices crosswise into thirds or halves depending on size of food to be wrapped. (It should overlap slightly).
2. Secure overlapped bacon around food with a wooden toothpick.
3. These appetizers may be either baked or broiled. Broiling is slightly faster, but baking offers the advantage of less danger of burning.

   To broil: Place 3 inches from source of heat. When topside is crisp, turn and continue broiling until second side is crisp.

   To bake: Bake at 425°, until bacon is crisp. Turn once during baking.

4. Drain on paper towels.
5. Keep hot on electric tray.
6. If prepared in advance, they may be reheated in a 350° oven for 5 minutes, or until heated through.

Rumaki

Makes 16-20

1-5 ounce can water chestnuts
¼ cup soy sauce
4-5 slices bacon
Sugar

1. Drain water chestnuts. Marinate in soy sauce several hours.
2. Cut water chestnuts in half if very large. Roll in sugar.
3. Cut bacon slices in half crosswise and again lengthwise.
4. Wrap water chestnuts in bacon slices. Secure with a toothpick.
5. Bake at 425° until bacon is crisp. Turn once.
6. Drain on paper towels.

May be made day before. Refrigerate. Before serving, reheat 10 minutes at 350°. Serve in chafing dish.

Broiled Stuffed Dates

Dates (seeds removed) Sherry
Chopped nuts Bacon
Cream cheese or cheddar cheese

1. Soak dried dates in sherry at least 36 hours.
2. Split and fill with nuts or cream cheese or a combination of both, or stuff with Cheddar cheese.
3. Wrap 1/3 slice bacon around fruit tightly to seal in filling and secure with toothpick.
4. Broil or bake until bacon is crisp.

Suggestion: Prunes can be substitued for dates.

Bacon Wrapped Water Chestnuts and Pineapple

Bacon slices, cut in thirds
Water chestnut slices
Drained canned pineapple chunks

1. Wrap a bacon slice around a chunk of pineapple and a slice of water chestnut and secure with a toothpick.
2. Broil or bake until bacon is crisp, turning once.
3. Drain on paper towels.
4. May be reheated on a rack in a shallow baking pan in a preheated 350° oven for 5 minutes.

Brazil Nuts in Bacon

Brazil nuts 2 tablespoons butter
Bacon strips cut ½ or 1/3
Salt

1. Melt butter in pan and saute' nuts until golden brown, remove pan from heat and salt nuts lightly.
2. Wrap bacon around nut and secure with toothpick.
3. Broil until bacon is crisp, turning often.

Artichoke Hearts and Bacon Tidbits

1 can artichoke hearts, drained
Onion powder
Bacon strips, cut in thirds.

1. Cut artichoke hearts in half and sprinkle with onion powder.
2. Wrap bacon slice around artichoke heart and secure with a toothpick.
3. Bake or broil until bacon is crisp, turning once.

Bacon-Watermelon Rinds

Bacon
Watermelon rind slices

1. Wrap ½ slices of bacon around bite sized pieces of watermelon rind. Fasten with toothpicks.
2. Bake at 425° until bacon is crisp. Turn once.

These tidbits can be prepared ahead and refrigerated and baked at serving time.

Stuffed Prune Broil

Makes 16

16 pitted prunes (preferably large)   8 slices of bacon
16 chunks of pineapple   Sherry wine to cover prunes

1. Soak prunes several days in Sherry.
2. Stuff one chunk pineapple in each prune.
3. Stretch ½ slice bacon and wrap around prune.
4. Secure bacon with toothpick.
5. Broil slowly about 300° until bacon is well cooked, not crisp. (Serve hot).

Note: Unused can be frozen, and water chestnuts (split) can be substituted for pineapple.

Bacon Wrapped Prune and Cheese Canapes

Seedless prunes   Teriyaki sauce
Aged Cheddar cheese
Bacon strips

1. Slit open prunes.
2. Fill with cheddar cheese cubes, cut 6 to the ounce.
3. Wrap with ½ slice bacon tightly to seal in cheese. Fasten with toothpick.
4. Sprinkle with Teriyaki sauce. Refrigerate several hours or overnight.
5. Bake at 425° until bacon is crisp. Turn once.

These are an instant hit. Your guest will never guess what the secret ingredients are.

Bacon Wrapped Scallops

Fresh bay or sea scallops   Teriyaki sauce
Bacon strips

1. Wash and drain scallops. Cut large ones in half.
2. Marinate scallops in Teriyaki sauce several hours or overnight.
3. Wrap in ½ strip of bacon. Secure with toothpick.
4. Sprinkle with additional Teriyaki sauce.
5. Bake at 425° until bacon is crisp, turning once.

Angels on Horseback

Oysters, fresh or frozen
Bacon slices, cut in half or thirds
Salt, pepper, paprika

1. Season fresh oysters (or thawed frozen ones) with salt, pepper and paprika.
2. Wrap bacon slice around oyster and secure with toothpick.
3. Broil or bake slowly until crisp. turning once.

Frankfurters, Cheese and Bacon

Cocktail frankfurters
Cheddar cheese
Bacon strips, cut in thirds

1. Split cocktail frankfurter and insert a piece of Cheddar cheese.
2. Wrap with a third slice of bacon tightly to seal in cheese and secure with a toothpick.
3. Bake at 350° for about 20 minutes, or until bacon is crisp.

Broiled Olives in Bacon

Large stuffed olives
Bacon slices, cut in halves or thirds.

1. Wrap olives with bacon and secure with toothpick.
2. Broil, turning occasionally, until bacon is crisp. Drain on absorbent paper.

Blini with Sour Cream and Caviar

2 eggs
1 medium onion, quartered
1 teaspoon salt

2 cups diced raw potatoes
¼ cup flour
¼ cup parsley clusters

1. Into blender container, put eggs, onion, salt, parsley, and half of diced potatoes. Cover container and turn motor on high.
2. Uncover container, and with motor on, add flour and remaining half of potatoes. As soon as last cube of potato is added turn off motor.
3. Fry tiny pancakes (half-dollar size) in ¼ inch deep hot fat. Turn when light brown on bottom. Remove when second side is light brown.
4. Drain very well on paper towels.
5. When cold, pack on an aluminum foil tray, waxed paper between layers. Wrap for freezer.
6. At time of use, heat in 450° oven. When hot and brown, drain well on paper towels, serve with bowls of caviar and sour cream.

Pick a rainy day when you have nothing else to do. Make lots! They freeze well and will keep for several months. They can be removed from freezer in any needed quantity. Instant elegance!

Petite Potato Pancakes

2 cups raw grated potatoes
2 eggs beaten well
1 tablespoon flour

⅛ teaspoon baking powder
½ grated onion
Dash pepper
1½ teaspoons salt

1. Grate potatoes and drain well, pressing out excess water.
2. Add remaining ingredients and blend thoroughly.
3. Drop from tablespoon into well-greased frying pan. Brown on both sides.
4. Set aside. Reheat in 350° oven for 10 minutes.

Serve with sour cream and caviar. Makes about 30 cocktail-size pancakes.

May be made through step 3 and heated when ready to serve.

Brandeis Special

1 package small party rye bread
Thin slices Kosher salami
Russian dressing

Slices processed Swiss cheese
(each cut into 4 squares)

1. Spread a little Russian dressing on one side of rye bread slice.
2. Place a slice of salami on bread and top with ¼ square of cheese.
3. Bake in 350° oven until cheese is melted and salami sizzles a little.

COLD
PICKUPS

5

Lox Pinwheels

½ pound lox (smoked salmon)
4 ounces whipped cream cheese
1 teaspoon chives
1 dozen miniature bagels, split and buttered

1. Mix cream cheese and chives.
2. Spread mixture on lox; roll up like a jelly roll.
3. Wrap tightly in waxed paper. Refrigerate at least 4 hours.
4. Slice crosswise to give a pinwheel effect.

Serve on bagel. Everything can be done in the a.m. but do not place lox mixture on bagel until last minute.

Anchovy Canapés

Makes 20 canapes

6 tablespoons butter
2 tablespoons anchovy paste
20 artichoke hearts
8 ounces whipped cream cheese
20 bread rounds

1. Blend butter and anchovy paste.
2. Spread rounds with anchovy butter.
3. Ring outer edge with cream cheese.
4. In center place artichoke heart and dot of pimiento.

Shrimp Cheese Balls

Makes about 3½ dozen

1-8 ounce package cream cheese,
   thoroughly creamed
1½ teaspoons prepared mustard
1 teaspoon grated onion
1 teaspoon lemon juice
Dash of cayenne pepper

4½ ounce can (¾ cup)
   shrimp, drained
2/3 cup chopped salted
   mixed nuts
Dash of salt

1. Soften cream cheese.
2. Blend in mustard, onion, lemon juice, cayenne pepper and salt.
3. Break shrimp into pieces; stir into cheese mixture. Chill.
4. Form into ½-inch balls, and roll in chopped nuts.

Bologna Wedges

1-3 ounce package cream cheese
1 tablespoon horseradish
2 tablespoons cream

½ teaspoon MSG
6 slices bologna

1. Combine cheese, horseradish, cream and Accent.
2. Spread on five slices of bologna. Stack together and top with one unspread slice.
3. Chill until cheese is hard. Slice wedges for hors d'oeuvres.

Delicious with Kosher bologna.

Corned Beef Canapés

1 cucumber, chopped and drained
3 ounces cream cheese
Corned beef, sliced thin

1. Mix finely chopped cucumber with 3 ounces softened cream cheese.
2. Spread on small slices corned beef.
3. Roll up tightly; wrap in waxed paper. Chill ½ hour before serving.

Also good with ham or smoked salmon.

Salami Sardine Canapé

¼ pound hard salami, thinly sliced
1 can skinless boneless sardines, drained
1 tablespoon mayonnaise
Bread slices

1. Mash sardines; mix with mayonnaise.
2. Spread on slice of salami and roll up.
3. Cut bread slices to fit salami roll.
4. Butter bread and place roll on top, seam side down.

Pickled Dog

Ring bologna
Distilled vinegar
2 tablespoons pickling spices
1 red pepper

1. Cut bologna into bite-sized cubes.
2. Pack gently into quart jar.
3. Add pickling spices and red pepper.
4. Fill jar with vinegar. Put lid on jar.
5. Refrigerate for 24 hours before using.

A specialty of Hedrick's General Store, Nashville, Indiana.

This is a great picnic hors d'oeuvre. Serve with toothpicks.

Curried Chicken Balls

Makes 5 dozen

1-8 ounce package cream cheese,
    thoroughly creamed
4 tablespoons mayonnaise
2 cups chopped cooked chicken
1½ cups chopped almonds
3 tablespoons chopped chutney
1 teaspoon salt
2 teaspoons curry powder
1 cup grated coconut

1. Blend cheese and mayonnaise.
2. Sauté almonds in 1 tablespoon butter until lightly browned.
3. Add almonds, chicken, chutney, salt and curry powder to cream cheese mixture.
4. Shape into walnut sized balls. Roll each ball in coconut. Chill until ready to serve.

These can be frozen. Serve with large colored toothpicks.

Prosciutto and Asparagus

1. Drain canned asparagus, wrap a small piece of Prosciutto around, fasten with toothpick. Serve cold.

Prosciutto and Melon

1. Make 1 inch cantaloupe cubes.
2. Wrap a small piece of Prosciutto around each cube. Fasten with a toothpick. Serve cold.

Approximately 20 calories per piece.

Cheese-Fruit Appetizers

1. Spear a cube of sharp Cheddar cheese and a grape, mandarin orange section or a pineapple chunk with a toothpick. Walnut or pecan halves are also good with cheese.

Cheese-Nut Appetizers

1. Mash together equal quantities of butter and Roquefort or Bleu cheese.
2. Spread a little mixture between two walnut halves; chill.

Deviled Cream Cheese Balls

Makes 30 cream cheese balls

1-8 ounce pkg. cream cheese
1-8¾ ounce can pineapple
   tidbits, drained

Chopped parsley or chives
1-2¼ ounce can deviled ham

1. Blend cream cheese and deviled ham. Chill.
2. Place pineapple tidbits on paper towels to drain well. Cut each piece in half crosswise.
3. Roll a spoonful of cheese mixture around each pineapple piece to form a 1-inch ball. Chill.
4. Roll in chopped parsley or chives when ready to serve.

Serve with toothpicks.

Deviled Eggs

General instructions for deviled eggs

To boil eggs:
1. Prick one end of egg with a pin to prevent cracking.
2. Place eggs gently in saucepan, cover with cold water.
3. Bring to boil; reduce heat to keep water simmering and continue to cook for 15 minutes.
4. Pour off boiling water and let cold tap water run over eggs until cool enough to handle.
5. Remove shell and slice eggs in half. They can be sliced either lengthwise or crosswise. To make crosswise cut eggs stand on platter, trim off a small slice of egg white from rounded end.
6. Stuff eggs with filling of your choice. They may be garnished with paprika, curry powder, a slice of stuffed green olive, a slice of pimiento, a caper, a rolled anchovy, red or black caviar. Choose garnish to harmonize with filling.
7. To prepare fillings: Remove egg yolks. Mash and combine with all remaining ingredients except garnishes. Refill egg whites. Pastry tube can be used, if desired, for decorative effect.
8. Deviled eggs may be prepared a day or two ahead and stored in refrigerator, wrapped air tight with Saran wrap. Add garnish a few hours before serving.

Deviled Egg Fillings For 6 Eggs

Basic Deviled Eggs

Makes 12 halves

6 egg yolks
* ¼ cup mayonnaise
¼ teaspoon salt
Dash freshly ground pepper
2 teaspoons prepared mustard

1 tablespoon finely chopped celery
1 tablespoon finely chopped stuffed green olives
1 tablespoon finely chopped green onion

Pink Deviled Eggs

12 egg yolks
1 can (7¾ ounces) salmon, drained
* ½ cup mayonnaise
1 tablespoon minced pimiento
1 teaspoon grated onion
1 teaspoon dry mustard

Salt and pepper to taste
Few drops Tabasco
Parsley for garnish

* *Note: The amount of mayonnaise will depend on the size of the eggs; add sparingly with small eggs.*

Anchovy-Stuffed Eggs

6 egg yolks
1 teaspoon anchovy paste
* 3 tablespoons mayonnaise
1 teaspoon sugar

1 tablespoon finely chopped
parsley or 1 teaspoon
dehydrated

Sardine Stuffed Eggs

6 egg yolks
1-4⅜ ounce boneless,
skinless oil packed
sardines, drained

* 3-4 tablespoons mayonnaise
Morton's Nature Seasoning
Blend (to taste)
2 teaspoons lemon juice

Smoked Salmon Stuffed Eggs

6 egg yolks
4 ounces smoked salmon
finely chopped (½ cup)
* ¼ cup mayonnaise
¼ teaspoon salt

Dash freshly ground pepper
Drained black olive and
pimiento to garnish
1 tablespoon chopped parsley, or
1 teaspoon dehydrated

Deviled Ham and Eggs

6 egg yolks
1 can (2¼ ounces) deviled ham
¼ teaspoon Worcestershire sauce
1 tablespoon prepared mustard

3 drops onion juice
* 1-3 tablespoons mayonnaise
(enough to moisten)
Salt
White pepper

Crab Meat Eggs

12 hard-cooked eggs
1 cup cooked flaked crab meat
½ cup minced celery
½ cup chopped almonds

2 tablespoons minced green pepper
* Mayonnaise to moisten
1 teaspoon prepared mustard
¼ teaspoon salt

*Note: May be made with tuna fish. The crunchy texture of almonds
and the tasty crabmeat will surprise and delight your guests.*

* (see note page 87)

Chicken-Stuffed Eggs

6 egg yolks
½ cup minced chicken
  breast
¼ cup chopped celery
1 teaspoon prepared mustard
1-2 tablespoons sour cream

* 2 tablespoons mayonnaise
2 tablespoons chopped
  pistachio nuts
Salt and pepper to taste
Paprika to garnish

Chicken Deviled Eggs

6 egg yolks
½ cup minced chicken (or turkey)
4 drops onion juice
1 teaspoon anchovy paste
3 drops lemon juice

* 1-3 tablespoons mayonnaise
  (enough to moisten)
Salt and pepper

Garnish with rolled anchovy fillet (with caper in center).

Chutney Eggs

6 egg yolks
3 slices crisp cooked,
  crumbled bacon

* 1-2 tablespoons mayonnaise
3 tablespoons finely
  chopped chutney, drained

Deviled Eggs - Low Calorie

6 warm, hard cooked eggs
¼ teaspoon salt
¼ teaspoon dry mustard

¼ cup plain yogurt
½ teaspoon Worcestershire sauce
1 teaspoon lemon juice
Parsley

Artichoke Deviled Eggs

6 egg yolks
1 package frozen artichoke hearts
1 to 2 tablespoons whipped
  sweet butter
2 teaspoons lemon juice

¼ cup wine vinegar
¼ cup olive oil
1 teaspoon salt
¼ teaspoon freshly ground black
  pepper

1. Cook frozen artichoke hearts according to package directions, drain and cool. Cut each in half.
2. Marinate in a mixture of wine vinegar, olive oil, salt and black pepper for at least 4 hours. Drain well.
3. Mash egg yolks while still warm and add whipped sweet butter and lemon juice mixing well.
4. Put artichoke half in each egg white and pile the yolk mixture high on top.

* (see note page 87)

89

Mushroom Stuffed Eggs Russian-style

Makes 16 halves

8 eggs
4 ounces mushrooms (canned)
1 small onion, minced

2 teaspoons salt butter
6 teaspoons mayonnaise
4 teaspoons sour cream
Salt, pepper, to taste
Pinch of cayenne
Pimiento
Parsley

1. Slice cooled hard boiled eggs in half and remove yolks and mash.
2. In melted butter, fry onion and chopped mushrooms.
3. Mix onion, mushroom mixture with mashed egg yolks and season with salt, pepper and cayenne. If necessary, add a little mayonnaise to bind mixture.
4. Stuff egg whites, mounding the filling.
5. Mix mayonnaise and sour cream together and spoon onto stuffed eggs.
6. Garnish with pimiento pieces and chopped parsley.

FILLED CREAM PUFFS

Chicken Puffs

Makes 3½ dozen small puffs

2 cups finely chopped,
  cooked chicken
¼ cup finely chopped celery
2 tablespoons chopped pimiento
1/3 cup mayonnaise or
  salad dressing
¼ teaspoon salt

Dash pepper
2/3 cup water
1 stick pie crust mix,
  crumbled
2 eggs
2 tablespoons dry white wine

1. In mixer bowl, stir together chicken, celery, pimiento, mayonnaise, wine, salt, and pepper; chill.
2. In small saucepan, heat water to boiling. Add crumbled pie crust mix; stir well over low heat till pastry forms a ball and leaves sides of pan. Cool 1 minute more, stirring constantly.
3. Add eggs and beat on low speed of electric mixer for 2 minutes.
4. Drop dough from rounded teaspoon onto ungreased baking sheet. Bake in 425° oven for 20 to 25 minutes till puffed, golden brown and dry.
5. Transfer puffs to rack; cool slowly away from drafts.
6. Split and fill with chilled chicken mixture.

Can be used for a luncheon. Makes 12 luncheon-sized puffs. Drop dough from rounded tablespoon onto baking sheet; bake 25 minutes.

Duchesses
Tiny Cream Puffs

½ cup butter
⅛ teaspoon salt
1 cup boiling water
1 cup sifted flour
3 eggs (unbeaten)

1. Add butter and salt to boiling water and stir over medium heat until mixture boils.
2. Reduce heat, add flour all at once and beat vigorously until mixture leaves the sides of pan.
3. Remove from heat and add 1 egg at a time, beating thoroughly after each addition.
4. Shape puffs very small, using about 1 teaspoon paste for each one.
5. On greased cookie sheet bake in a very hot oven (450°) for about 8 minutes or until points begin to brown, then reduce heat to moderate (350°) and continue baking 10 to 12 minutes longer.
6. When cold, cut tops from duchesses, fill lower half and press top over filling.

Fillings For Cream Puffs

Cream Cheese and Ham

6 ounces cream cheese, softened   Catsup to moisten.
1-2¼ ounce can deviled ham

Blend well.

Cream Cheese and Roquefort

3 ounces cream cheese   Dry sherry to moisten
Roquefort cheese to taste

Blend well.

Shrimp Filling

1 can frozen shrimp soup, thawed
2 heaping tablespoons sour cream

Blend well.

Additional Fillings

Chopped chicken salad, tuna fish or egg salad or any favorite spread filling.

MEATY
SUBJECTS

6

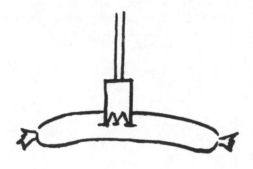

Grilled Flank Steak

½ cup salad oil
¼ cup soy sauce
2 tablespoons vinegar
1 teaspoon powdered ginger

¾ teaspoon garlic salt
3 tablespoons honey
Flank steak

1. Combine first 6 ingredients.
2. Pour over steak and marinate overnight, turning several times.
3. Remove from marinade.
4. Cook briefly over charcoal (meat should be rare).
5. Slice in thin strips, cutting across grain. Serve on miniature buns as hors d'oeuvre.

For a variation, use the following for marinade, using above procedure.

¼ cup olive oil
¼ cup soy sauce
½ cup red wine
1 clove garlic, crushed

1 onion, sliced thin
1 teaspoon ginger
Salt and pepper to taste

Grilled Beef Strips

Makes about 20

1 pound round steak,
    about 1" thick
1 clove garlic, thinly sliced
2 tablespoons Sherry
1 teaspoon sugar

1/3 cup soy sauce
1" piece of fresh ginger, thinly sliced or 1 teaspoon ground ginger

1. Remove fat from meat and slice very thin. (It is easier to do if meat is partially frozen.)
2. Mix remaining ingredients and marinate meat strips in mixture for at least ½ hour.
3. Thread meat on wooden sticks and broil over hot coals on grill or hibachi.

Steak Tartare I

This is a recipe that makes a hit when served at cocktail parties. It is a slight variation on what is usually done to season ground beef. It was obtained from a gourmet who lost his teeth and ate nothing but steak tartare every night for dinner. No anchovies are included because I don't like them. The recipe calls for Mr. Mustard which is the way it was given to me. It won't work with any other type mustard other than a dijon or dijon style. The two dijon style mustards made in the U.S.A. are Mr. Mustard and Grey Poupon. A true French dijon would be great but by the time it gets to the shelves in this country it has lost its flavor. A pound of this recipe is adequate for an hors d'oeuvre but might only serve two or three as a main course. This recipe for two pounds can be used at a large cocktail party.

2 pounds ground round steak
3-4 teaspoons Dijon mustard
1 tablespoon chili sauce
1½ tablespoons half and half
  (or cream)
1 small onion finely grated
Salt
Ground black pepper

Garlic powder
Dill weed
MSG
Capers
Parsley flakes
Paprika

1. Place the meat in a mixing bowl and make a large crater in the center. Put in the mustard, chili sauce, half and half, and the grated onion as shown above. Sprinkle in to taste some salt, pepper and optionally garlic powder, dill weed and MSG. Take a wooden spoon and carefully mix the ingredients into the meat until it is uniformly spread throughout.
2. Place on a serving platter(it can be round or long like a meat loaf.)
3. Garnish the top with parsley flakes, paprika, (both for color) and with capers.

The capers may be placed in a side dish so they can be used optionally if desired. Serve with party rye, melba toast rounds or any other type of bread or cracker.

Steak Tartare II

2 pounds top round, ground
  three times
1 raw egg
Dash A-1 sauce
1 teaspoon salt
½ teaspoon hot sauce

½ teaspoon fresh ground pepper
½ bottle chili sauce
½ cup chopped sweet onion
1 can anchovies

1. Mix first seven ingredients together.
2. Place on serving platter and garnish with anchovies.

Note: Serve with party rye and chopped onions in a bowl on the side.

Appetizer Ranch Ribs

Serves 6

2/3 tablespoon Karo all-purpose syrup
2 tablespoons corn starch
1/3 cup soy sauce
2 tablespoons Worcestershire sauce
1 teaspoon ginger

¼ cup vinegar
1 clove garlic, crushed
¼ teaspoon salt
½ cup light brown sugar
Dash of Tabasco sauce

1. Cook above ingredients for five minutes.
2. Have butcher crack 4 pounds spare ribs into two inch long pieces.
3. Prior to cooking, cut apart and separate into ribs.
4. Simmer in pot of water to cover, add one onion and cook until tender but meat still clings to bone.
5. Drain ribs and chill. Can be made as long as two days before and kept in refrigerator.
6. When ready to bake place ribs on rack in large pan, and brush with the sauce.
7. Pour sauce over ribs in pan, place in 325° oven. Bake for 1½ hours or until tender and glazed, basting often.

Serving Suggestions: Serve part at a time. Keep remaining hot for platter refills leaving oven turned to slow 250°. Serve as is or with prepared horseradish to dip in.

Cocktail Spareribs

Serves 8

3 pounds spareribs cracked in 2-3" pieces
1 teaspoon MSG
3 tablespoons soy sauce
½ cup prepared mustard
1 cup brown sugar

1. Bake ribs at 325° for 1½ hours. Drain on paper towels.
2. Make sauce of remaining ingredients.
3. Brush ribs with sauce.
4. Return ribs to 300° oven, bake 45 minutes, basting several times.

MEATBALLS

In miniature the meatball is an easy, inexpensive, do-it-ahead hors d'oeuvre. For a main course shape larger meatballs.

Miniature Stuffed Cabbages

2 small cabbages
1 cup chopped onion
1 clove garlic
2-15 oz. cans Tomato Sauce
  with tomato bits
1 can water
Juice of 3 lemons
2/3 cup brown sugar

½ cup raisins
1 cup cooked rice (1/3 cup raw)
1½ pounds ground round
¼ c grated onion
1 teaspoon salt
⅛ teaspoon pepper
½-¾ cup ginger snaps, crumbled

1. Select small firm cabbages and boil until leaves become flexible enough to separate and roll. Set aside to cool.
2. In a large, heavy skillet saute onions, sliced clove of garlic. Add tomato sauce, water, lemon juice, brown sugar, raisins and salt and pepper to taste.
3. While sauce is cooking, prepare rice. Add raw ground round to cooked rice; add grated onion, salt and pepper to raw meat mixture.
4. Roll meat-rice mixture into cabbage leaves (make small). Secure with good quality wood toothpicks.
5. Place carefully into tomato sauce mixture and cook slowly for 2 or 3 hours.
6. Add ginger snaps about ½ hour before cabbages are done and then watch carefully for burning or sticking. (Mix crumbled ginger snaps with ¼ cup sauce; stir to blend well before pouring into sauce.)

Better made day ahead and refrigerated over night. Can be reheated in casserole dish in oven.

Russian Meat Balls

1 pound ground chuck
1 cup diced onion
1 teaspoon salt
⅛ teaspoon lemon pepper
¼ teaspoon paprika

1 egg
½ cup catsup or more as needed
2 tablespoons shortening
2 slices white bread

1. Saute onions in shortening.
2. Make crumbs out of bread and add to meat. Mix with 2 tablespoons catsup, egg, salt, paprika, and lemon pepper.
3. Shape into 20 meatballs. Place on top of onions. Sprinkle with additional salt, lemon pepper, paprika and remaining catsup. Simmer covered on low heat 1½ hours.

Meat Balls Stroganoff

½ cup chopped onion
1 tablespoon butter
½ pound sliced mushrooms
1 pound lean ground round
1 teaspoon salt
¼ teaspoon pepper
½ cup bread crumbs
3 ounces tomato paste

3 tablespoons bouillon
½ cup Sherry
1 Tablespoon Worcestershire
  sauce
1½ teaspoons celery salt
¼ cup sliced green pepper
1 cup sour cream

1. Sauté onion in butter. Set aside.
2. Sauté mushrooms in butter. Set aside.
3. Mix ground round, salt, pepper, and bread crumbs. Form into small meat balls.
4. Sauté meat balls till lightly browned or place on baking pan in 400° oven for 5 minutes.
5. Combine meatballs, onion, tomato paste, bouillon, Sherry, Worcestershire sauce, celery salt. Simmer 20 minutes. Add green pepper and simmer 10 minutes longer. Stir in sour cream and mushrooms and heat just to boiling point. (Do not boil sour cream, or it will curdle).

An inexpensive version of a gourmet recipe which usually uses steak as the meat. It may be prepared a day ahead. Heat and add sour cream when ready to serve.
Keep hot in chafing dish.

Meatballs in Potato-Dill Sauce

Serves 4-6

1 pound ground chuck
2 slices white bread, cubed
1½ cups milk
1 egg
2 tablespoons parsley
1 teaspoon salt

1 teaspoon pepper
2 tablespoons salad oil
2-10½ oz. cans condensed cream
  of potato soup
3 tablespoons dill weed

1. In medium bowl, place bread. Add ½ cup milk and let stand until milk is absorbed.
2. Stir in chuck, egg, parsley, and salt and pepper.
3. Shape into 1 inch balls. Brown in oil and drain on paper towels.
4. Meanwhile in medium saucepan over medium heat, heat un-diluted soup, remaining cup of milk, and dill weed until boiling. Add meatballs and heat through.

Make ahead. Refrigerate or freeze. Reheat. Serve in chafing dish.

Sauerkraut Balls with Delicate Mustard Sauce

1 pound lean, ground
   round beef
1-16 ounce can sauerkraut
½ cup frozen chopped onion

2 tablespoons flour
2 eggs
¾ cup mashed potatoes*
Italian seasoned bread crumbs

1. Drain sauerkraut; chop a little.
2. Mix meat, well-drained sauerkraut, and onion.
3. Add flour, eggs and potatoes; stir together.
4. Roll into 1 inch balls, then roll in crumbs.
5. Deep fry and serve hot with following Delicate Mustard Sauce.

Note: Can be made ahead and frozen. To freeze, place balls on waxed paper lined cookie sheet. When frozen solid, place balls in a plastic bag and return to freezer. Remove as needed and heat in a 350° oven on foil lined pan until heated through.

*¾ cup dehydrated potatoes that have been reconstituted according to directions on the package can be substituted for mashed potatoes.

Delicate Mustard Sauce

13¾ ounce can chicken broth
½ to 1 teaspoon Dijon mustard
   to taste

1 tablespoon lemon juice
3 eggs yolks

1. Place chicken broth in top half of double boiler and simmer over direct heat until broth is reduced to about half the quantity or 1¼ cups.
2. Beat egg yolks. Add lemon juice and ½ cup reduced broth stirring constantly with a wire whisk to avoid lumps.
3. Place top half of double boiler holding remaining chicken broth over bottom half of double boiler which has ½ inch of boiling water in it.
4. Gradually pour egg yolk mixture into remaining chicken broth stirring constantly with wire whisk. Continue heating and stirring until thickened (about 5 minutes). Remove from heat.
5. Add mustard to taste.

Note: When ready to serve, reheat sauce in double boiler. Serve sauerkraut balls with toothpicks. Dip in warm sauce to eat.

Dolmadakia Avgolemono
(Stuffed grape leaves with lemon sauce)

½ pound lean ground lamb
½ pound lean ground beef
1 teaspoon salt
½ teaspoon basil
2 tablespoons dehydrated onion
¼ teaspoon fresh
  ground pepper
¼ cup raw rice
2 teaspoons dill weed
1 tablespoon dehydrated parsely
1 egg
1 jar grape leaves

2 cups chicken broth
½ cup dry white wine
6 tablespoons lemon juice
Whole rind of lemon
1 clove garlic
1 stick cinnamon
4 egg yolks
1-2 teaspoons Wondra flour
  to thicken

1. Mix beef, lamb, salt, basil, onion, pepper, rice, dill weed, parsley and egg until well blended.
2. Rinse grape leaves. Drain on paper towels.
3. Place 1 tablespoon meat in center of each leaf; roll from stem end, tucking in edges to hold meat in place. Secure with a wooden toothpick.
4. Mix broth, wine, 3 tablespoons of lemon juice, lemon rind, garlic and cinnamon stick in pot. Place a layer of grape leaves on bottom of pot. Lay meat rolls in layers. Simmer for 1 hour, basting occasionally with sauce. Add more soup if necessary during cooking.
5. Remove rolls from broth; reserve broth. Place in bake and serve dish for reheating.
6. Strain broth, discarding lemon peel, garlic and cinnamon. Beat egg yolks and remaining 3 tablespoons lemon juice. Beat in hot broth. Cook in double boiler until thick, stirring frequently with wire whisk.

A piquant flavored, easily prepared dish. Delicious!
To serve:
    Cover meat rolls and heat in 300° oven until very hot. (They may be refrigerated or frozen and reheated.)

The sauce is best reheated over boiling water to prevent curdling and separating. It may be frozen but it should be stirred with a wire whisk when reheating.

Chinese Meat Balls

Makes 3 dozen

MEATBALLS
1 pound ground beef
1 egg
1 teaspoon salt
2 tablespoons chopped onion
Pepper
½ cup bread crumbs
¼ cup water

SAUCE
3 tablespoons cornstarch
1 tablespoon soy sauce
3 tablespoons vinegar
½ cup sugar
1 tablespoon oil
1½ cups pineapple juice
4 slices pineapple
1 green pepper
1 jar sliced pimiento

1. Mix together ingredients for meatballs.
2. Form into 36 small balls. Bake at 375° for 10 minutes, uncovered.
3. Mix cornstarch with soy sauce, vinegar, ¼ cup pineapple juice and sugar. Blend well to remove lumps. Add oil and remaining pineapple juice. Bring to boil, stirring frequently and cook 1 minute.
4. Cut pineapple and green pepper into chunks and add to sauce.
5. Add meatballs. Heat 'til meatballs are warmed through.

A great do it ahead recipe!

Meatballs may be baked and frozen ahead. Sauce may be made ahead, but add pineapple, green pepper and pimiento at time of reheating to serve. Serve piping hot in chafing dish.

*As a main course, add ½ cup sliced water chestnuts and 1 cup pea pods. Serve over rice.

Goody Meat Balls From the Chafing Dish

Serves about 20 if you serve something else

MEATBALLS
3 pounds ground beef (round if you can afford it)
2 cups Parmesan cheese, grated
5 eggs
2 teaspoons salt
⅛ teaspoon pepper
4 cloves garlic, minced
6 slices white bread soaked & squeezed
Enough olive oil to cover bottom of pan

SAUCE
2½ bottles catsup (14 ounce each)
2½ cups white wine

1. Mix meat, cheese, eggs, salt, pepper, garlic and bread.
2. Form meat balls (larger than a marble but smaller than a golf ball). Brown carefully in olive oil.
3. Make sauce of catsup and wine.
4. Simmer meatballs in sauce 10 minutes in chafing dish.

Make ahead. Refrigerate or freeze. Warm. Serve in chafing dish with toothpicks.

Sweet and Sour Meatballs I

Makes 30 appetizers

½ cup water
1/3 cup packed dark brown sugar
¼ cup lemon juice
1 tablespoon catsup
¾ pound ground round steak

1 egg
¼ cup bread crumbs
¼ teaspoon salt
Dash pepper

1. Combine water, brown sugar, lemon juice and catsup in saucepan. Heat to boiling.
2. In medium bowl, combine ground round, egg, bread crumbs, salt and pepper. Form into meatballs. Place in saucepan.
3. Cook, covered over low heat for 15 minutes.

Can be made ahead and frozen. Serve in chafing dish with toothpicks.

Sweet and Sour Meatballs II

3 pounds ground beef
2 cans jellied cranberry sauce (10 oz.)
2 bottles chili sauce

1 jar sauerkraut (32 oz.)
Brown sugar and lemon juice to taste
Pumpernickel bread, crumbled

1. Prepare ground beef with favorite recipe for meatball mixture and shape into small cocktail size meatballs.
2. In Dutch oven, combine cranberry sauce and chili sauce to blend, adding sauerkraut and juice and brown sugar and lemon juice to taste. Bring to a slow boil.
3. Add a few slices of pumpernickel bread to thicken sauce (about 3 slices).
4. Drop uncooked meatballs into sauce and cook slowly for one hour.

This recipe tastes better if prepared ahead of time and refrigerated overnight. Reheat to serve. Can also be frozen.

Meatballs and Cocktail Onions

Makes 24 meatballs

½ pound ground round (lean)
1 tablespoon grated Parmesan
    cheese
1 tablespoon catsup

½ teaspoon MSG
¾ teaspoon salt
Dash pepper
24 cocktail onions

1. Mix meat and seasonings.
2. Drain onions.
3. Make meat into balls with onions in center. Chill.
4. Bake at 450° for 5 minutes.

15 calories per meatball. Best rare.

Swedish Meat Balls

Serves 8 to 10

2 pounds ground chuck
2 eggs
1 tablespoon minced onion
1 tablespoon milk

1 can jellied cranberry sauce (10 oz.)
1 bottle chili sauce
1 bottle of water
   to empty chili sauce bottle
1 10 oz. can of sauerkraut

1. Combine meat, eggs, onion and milk. Make into small balls.
2. Mix cranberry sauce, chili sauce, water and drained sauerkraut.
3. Place layers of meat balls and sauce in casserole. Bake at 325° for 45 minutes. Stir once after 25 minutes.

Make ahead; Refrigerate. Reheat and serve in chafing dish.

Meat Balls Elmira

Sauce

8-oz. grape jelly
¾ cup water

1 bottle chili sauce
3 tablespoons lemon juice

* * * * * *

Meat Balls

2 pounds ground beef
½ cup milk
2 small onions, grated
2 eggs
½ teaspoon pepper

4 slices white bread
   with crust
2 tablespoons minced parsley
1 teaspoon salt

1. Combine sauce ingredients and simmer 30 minutes.
2. To make meat balls, tear bread; mix with milk to make paste. (mushy but not runny). Combine with rest of ingredients. (Cook one meat ball to test for flavor. Correct seasoning if necessary). Shape with teaspoon. Chill at least one hour. Sauté. Refrigerate until needed.
3. Add cooked meatballs to sauce and simmer another 30 minutes. If meat balls are cold, make sure sauce returns to boil before timing next 30 minutes.

Meat balls may be made ahead and frozen. Serve in chafing dish.

Alternate Sauce
1-10 ounce jar of apricot preserves
¼ cup hot barbecue sauce
3 tablespoons lemon juice
½ cup water

Wieners

Wiener Tidbits

2 large eggs, hard boiled
Grated onion or onion powder, to taste
Salt and pepper, to taste

Mayonnaise
1 package wieners

1. Peel eggs and chop. Combine with onion, salt, pepper, and enough mayonnaise to hold together.
2. Split each wiener lengthwise almost to the bottom. Fill them with the egg spread. Hold together with 1 or 2 wooden toothpicks.
3. Place on cookie sheet or pan.
4. Heat in 325° oven until heated through, 10-15 minutes.
5. Remove from oven and cut each wiener in 3 or 4 pieces.

Note: Serve warm on toothpicks. Can be made a few days ahead and refrigerated. Place in oven before serving. Wieners can also be filled with cream cheese and served cold.

Drunken Hot Dogs

Serves 6 to 8

1 pound cocktail franks
¾ cup Bourbon
1½ cups ketchup

½ cup brown sugar
1 tablespoon grated onion,
   (optional)

1. Mix all ingredients together in a saucepan.
2. Simmer over low heat for 1 hour. If it dries out, add little more bourbon.

Note: Transfer to chafing dish and serve with toothpicks.

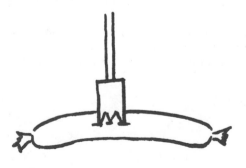

Sweet and Sour Sausages

Equal parts of currant jelly and prepared hot mustard
Wieners

1. Heat equal parts of jelly and mustard.
2. Broil wieners and cut into bite-sized portions.
3. Place wieners in jelly-mustard mix.

Serve in chafing dish with toothpicks.

Wieners in Sweet Sauce

Makes 2 cups sauce

1 (10 ounce) jar currant jelly
   or apple jelly
½ cup dark brown sugar,
   packed in cup
1 teaspoon dry mustard

1 teaspoon celery seed
1/3 cup cider vinegar
2 packages wieners
   or cocktail wieners

1. Combine first five ingredients and bring to a boil.
2. Cut wieners into bite size pieces. Heat in sauce.
3. Place heated wieners in sauce in chafing dish.

Note: Any leftover sauce may be refrigerated in a tightly covered jar
for more than a month and served again.

Cocktail Sausages and Mushrooms

Serves 5 to 6

1 can (8 ounce) tomato sauce
1 cup dry white wine
1 teaspoon garlic powder
1 teaspoon dried oregano

½ teaspoon salt
2 cans drained Vienna sausages
   (cut in half crosswise)
2 cans drained mushrooms caps

1. Combine tomato sauce, wine, and spices in saucepan. Simmer over low heat for five minutes.
2. Add sausages and mushrooms to sauce. Cover and simmer for twenty minutes.

Serve in chafing dish.

Duckling Paté

1 duck, quartered
3 cups water
2 teaspoons salt
10 peppercorns
1 bay leaf
4 cloves
1 teaspoon Worcestershire
  sauce

12 ounce can chopped black
  olives
½ cup sour cream
¼ teaspoon Tabasco
1 teaspoon salt
1 teaspoon grated onion
12 ounce cream cheese
1 can Sell's liver paté
¼ cup Brandy

1. Stew duck and giblets in water with salt, peppercorns, bay leaf and cloves, until tender. Let cool in broth ½ hour.
2. Pour off broth and let fat rise. (Reserve ¾ cup fat).
3. Put meat and giblets through on fine grinder of food chopper two times. (Discard skin).
4. Add remaining ingredients and ½ cup or less of reserved fat (enough to bind the paté).
5. Pack into tureen or small serving bowl. Pour remaining ¼ cup fat on top to seal.

A very luxurious paté. Worth getting greasy fingers. Chill before serving. Can be made a few days ahead. Don't freeze.

Chicken Fat

Throughout long and colorful history, Jewish tradition has been known for its steadfast faith, its respect for learning...and its chicken fat, otherwise known as "schmaltz". Melted over heat, with a bit of onion, chicken fat has lent its special deliciousness to everything from mashed potatoes to roast chicken. But its most popular and traditional use is in chopped chicken livers, where its mouth-watering flavor and light cohesiveness give the dish just the right consistency and taste. As an ancient sage once remarked, "Variations may come and go, but chopped liver without chicken fat is like a house without windows."

Chicken Fat Contemporary

1. Wash fat and drain on paper towels.
2. Place in cooking bag with 1 tablespoon frozen chopped onion per pound of chicken fat and 1 tablespoon flour.
3. Twist bag 2″ from top and fasten with twist tie.
4. Puncture 6 holes in top of bag.
5. Place bag in 2 inch deep baking pan a little larger than bag.
6. Bake at 275° for 45 minutes.
7. Remove from oven and cool to room temperature.
8. Pull corner of bag over edge of pan and snip with scissors. Then tip pan and pour fat into jar.

Pan should be large enough to contain entire contents of bag in case it should leak.

Rendered Chicken Fat

1 pound raw chicken fat   1 tablespoon salt
2 extra large onions, sliced

1. Cook all ingredients in heavy pot until fat is melted and onion brown.
2. Remove onion and cool. Strain.

Note: Store chicken fat in a jar in refrigerator. Can be kept for a long time. Can be frozen. This recipe is "like Grandma used to make."

Chopped Liver

Get a group of women talking about chopped liver... and for every 5 cooks, you'll have 8 opinions about which is the best recipe. Here are a few versions of "the only way!"

Chopped Chicken Livers

1 pound chicken livers
4 tablespoon rendered chicken fat
1½ cups chopped onions
3 hard-cooked egg yolks

1 teaspoon salt
¼ teaspoon freshly ground
   black pepper

1. Wash the livers and remove any discolored spots. Drain.
2. Heat 2 tablespoons fat in frying pan; brown the onions in it. Remove the onions.
3. Cook the livers in the fat remaining in the skillet for 10 minutes.
4. Grind or chop the onions, liver and egg yolks until you have a smooth mixture.
5. Add the salt, pepper and remaining fat.
6. Mix and taste for seasoning.

Note: Serve cold with crackers as a spread or on lettuce as an appetizer.

Chopped Liver Contemporary

1 pound chicken livers
1 tablespoon flour
1 teaspoon salt
½ cup chopped frozen onions

6 hard boiled eggs
4 tablespoons chicken fat
¼ teaspoon pepper

1. Wash livers and drain on paper towels. Place livers in cooking bag with onions and 1 tablespoon chicken fat and flour.
2. Close bag with twist tie and make six ½″ slits in top of bag. Place bag in 2″ deep pan a little larger than bag.
3. Bake 30 minutes at 325° or until livers are no longer pink.
4. Drain livers and discard liquid.
5. Chop or grind the livers, onions and eggs to desired consistency.
6. Add salt, pepper and remaining 3 tablespoons chicken fat. Mix and taste for seasonings.

Mock Paté de Foie Gras

1 pound chicken livers
1 teaspoon salt
¼ teaspoon nutmeg
⅛ teaspoon ground cloves

1½ teaspoon dry mustard
4 tablespoons minced onions
1 teaspoon anchovy paste
Chicken fat (p. 108)

1. Cook livers in water barely to cover, about 20 minutes. Drain.
2. Put through fine blade of food chopper twice.
3. Add all remaining ingredients except chicken fat and mix well. Blend in sufficient softened chicken fat to bind.
4. Pack in mold and chill for several hours or overnight.

To serve: Unmold on serving tray,, decorate with two hard boiled eggs pressed through a sieve. Serve with party rye bread.

Chicken Liver Paté I

1 pound chicken livers
8 eggs, hard boiled
2-4 tablespoons chicken
   fat (p. 108)

1 medium to large size raw onion
Salt and pepper, to taste

1. Boil chicken livers till just done. Drain.
2. When cool, put liver, eggs and onion through grinder.
3. Add salt and pepper to taste and enough chicken fat to hold paté together.
4. Put in a mold.

Note: Serve with small party rye rounds or crackers. Can be made a day ahead.

Mushroom - Chicken Liver Paté

Serves 3 Cups

¼ cup butter
½ pound fresh mushrooms, sliced
1 pound chicken livers
1 teaspoon garlic salt
1 teaspoon paprika

1/3 cup finely chopped green onions
½ cup white table wine
3 drops Tabasco
½ cup butter
Salt

1. Saute for 5 min. in ¼ cup of butter — the mushrooms, livers, garlic salt, paprika and onion.
2. Add wine and Tabasco; cover and cook slowly for 5-10 minutes longer.
3. Cool; whirl in blender, blend in ½ cup of butter (softened) and salt to taste.
4. Turn into dish; chill overnight.
5. Unmold; garnish with parsley and thin lemon slices.

110

Chicken Liver Mousse

1 pound chicken livers	1 small onion
1½ teaspoons salt	Few sprigs parsley
½ teaspoon pepper	1 pint whipping cream (16 oz.)
2 eggs	1 cup jellied consommé
2 egg yolks	1 teaspoon gelatin
	¼ cup Sherry

1. Place all but last three ingredients in blender, in two installments (half at a time). Blend till smooth, combine and mix together.
2. Place in greased bake and serve dish. Place dish in pan of hot water. Bake 50 minutes at 350°. Cool.
3. Soften gelatin in sherry. Add to boiling consommé and stir until dissolved. Chill until partially set.
4. Pour over cooled liver mousse. Decorate with olives.

Suggestions: Serve with crackers to spread. Delicious! Nobody will guess that it takes only a few minutes to prepare.

Chicken Liver Paté II

1 pound chicken livers	1 tablespoon Worcestershire
1 small onion	sauce
¾ cup chicken stock	¼ teaspoon pepper
½ teaspoon each curry and paprika	¾ cup butter
1 teaspoon salt	Canned consomme (with gelatin)

1. Simmer livers and onion in stock five minutes. Drain.
2. Pour all ingredients into blender, except butter and consommé. Whirl until smooth.
3. Add butter a little at a time.
4. Put into dish and chill.
5. Pour consomme' over top. Chill till consomme' is jelled.

Make 1 day ahead.

Paté

1 teaspoon Knox gelatin
½ can undiluted consommé
1 large can Sell's liver pate

2-3 ounce packages
  cream cheese
2 tablespoons lemon juice
Worcestershire sauce
Lawry's seasoned salt

1. Soften gelatin in ¼ cup cold consomme. Add to remaining consomme, heated to boiling.
2. Pour thin layer in small mold. Refrigerate until hard.
3. Mix paté, cream cheese and lemon juice. Season to taste with Worcestershire and Lawry's seasoned salt.
4. Spread into mold, on top of jelled consommé.
5. Pour remaining consommé over paté
6. Refrigerate overnight.

Liver Paté

Makes 2½ cups

1 pound liverwurst
⅛ teaspoon dried thyme leaves
1 tablespoon Worcestershire
  sauce
⅛ teaspoon mace
1 teaspoon ground cloves

¼ cup soft butter or margarine
1½ tablespoons Sherry
1 tablespoon grated onion
¼ teaspoon pepper

1. Peel casing from liverwurst. In medium bowl, mash meat with fork until smooth.
2. Add remaining ingredients, except butter; mix well.
3. Blend in butter until well combined.
4. Pack into serving dish. Cover tightly; refrigerate until ready to use.

Serve with crackers or small slices of rye bread.

Chicken Livers in Brandy

Serves 8

2 pounds chicken livers
1 stick butter or margarine
3-4 tablespoons brown sugar

1 tablespoon lemon juice
1½ jiggers (1½ ounces) Cognac,
  Brandy or Sherry

1. Melt shortening. Add brown sugar and lemon juice. Add liquor.
2. Sauté chicken livers in skillet over medium heat until medium done, cover and keep warm at low heat. Do not allow them to dry out; they will get tough.

Note: Serve hot. Skewer on tooth picks. Use nice big chicken livers.

FISHING FOR COMPLIMENTS

7

COLD SEAFOODS
Herring Salad

10 to 12 Servings

1-16 ounce can red beets, drained
2-16 ounce jars of herring
  in wine sauce, drained
1 small can of sliced potatoes, drained
1 hard cooked egg
1 dill pickle

1 apple
½ pint sour cream
½ cup chopped almonds
1 tablespoon sugar

1. Cut first six ingredients into small cubes.
2. Mix sour cream with brine and onions from herring jar and add sugar and almonds; mix salad well.

Add wine sauce for desired consistency.

Note: An old German recipe. Put in a salad bowl; surround tray with slices of rye bread.

Seviche

Serves 8

1 pound raw scallops
1/3 cup lime juice
½ teaspoon salt
½ teaspoon MSG

2 teaspoons prepared mustard
½ cup chopped onion
1 hot red pepper, chopped

1. Put raw scallops in collander, pour boiling water over them and drain throughly. Place in bowl with lime juice, salt, MSG, mustard, chopped onion and red pepper. Let stand at least 3 hours, stirring occasionally. Drain on paper towels.

Serve cold with cocktail sauce. For a milder version, omit onion and pepper. 66 calories per serving.

Artichoke Bottoms - Crab Meat

Serves 6
6 artichoke bottoms
1-2 teaspoons mayonnaise

* 1-6 ounce can crabmeat

1. Mix drained crabmeat with mayonnaise.
2. Place on top of drained artichoke bottoms.
3. Garnish with capers or parsley.

Elegant & Easy

*(See page 26)

115

Pickled Shrimp Jamaica

Serves 12

1 cup dry white table wine
½ cup salad oil
4 tablespoons garlic-flavored
    wine vinegar
1 teaspoon seasoned salt

½ teaspoon dried dill weed
4 drops Tabasco Sauce
Dash Jamaica allspice
6 cups large cooked,cooled
    shelled shrimp

1. Mix first seven ingredients.
2. Pour over shrimps.
3. Refrigerate several hours or overnight.

Pickled Shrimp

2½ pounds fresh or frozen
    shrimp
½ cup celery tops
¼ cup mixed pickling spices
3½ teaspoons salt
2 cups sliced onions
7 or 8 bay leaves

PICKLING MARINADE
1¼ cups salad oil
¾ cup white vinegar
3 tablespoons capers
    and juice
2½ teaspoons salt
Dash Tabasco

1. Cover shrimp with boiling water. Add celery, spices and salt. Return to boiling point. Remove from heat and let stand, covered in boiling water 5 minutes. Then drain, cool with cold water.
2. Alternate shrimp and onion in a shallow dish.. Add the bay leaves.
3. Mix ingredients of pickling marinade. Pour over the shrimp and onions. Cover with plastic wrap and chill at least 24 hours in pickling marinade.

Note: Transfer shrimp, onion and marinade to serving dish when ready to serve. Have shrimp forks and small dishes available for service. Everyone asks for this recipe.

The shrimp in marinade can be kept at least a week in the refrigerator. Cover with Saran wrap.

Marinated Shrimp

3 pounds shrimp
3 pints mayonnaise

Juice from 1½ lemons
1 cup sliced red onion

1. Peel and cook shrimp.
2. Marinate with onion overnight in mixture of mayonnaise, lemon juice. Taste should be tart; add more lemon juice, if necessary.

Shrimp La Maz

½ cup mayonnaise
½ cup chili sauce
2 tablespoons pickle relish
1 tablespoon chopped pimiento
1 teaspoon green pepper, chopped

1 teaspoon chopped celery
1 chopped hard boiled egg
1 teaspoon prepared mustard
1 teaspoon Worcestershire sauce
2 pounds cooked shrimp.

1. Mix all ingredients except shrimp to make sauce. (This may be done 24 hours ahead of time).
2. Several hours before serving, combine with cooked shrimp.

Serve in large salad bowl with plates and forks.

This recipe is very similar to the delicious appetizer served by the famous Patio La Maz in Palm Beach, Florida. If any of the sauce remains after serving, it makes a very good dressing on a wedge of head lettuce.

HOT SEAFOODS

Crab and Almond Hors d'oeuvre

4 tablespoons butter
* 1 pound crab meat
2/3 cup slivered almonds, sauteed

1/3 cup heavy cream
3 tablespoons finely chopped
  fresh parsley
Salt & pepper

1. Melt butter in chafing dish. Add crabmeat; cook 5 minutes until delicately browned.
2. Add almonds, cream and parsley. Season with salt and pepper to taste. Cook 2 minutes longer.

Serve with toast rounds.

This may also be served in individual shells as a first course. Make ahead and place in shells. Reheat at 300° for 30 minutes or until well warmed.

*(See page 26)

Baked Minced Clams

Serves 4-6

3 tablespoons butter
  or margarine
½ cup chopped onions
2 cans minced clams

3 tablespoons mayonnaise
  (more if you like)
6 tablespoons seasoned
  bread crumbs
3 tablespoons dried parsley
  flakes

1. Sauté onions in butter.
2. Add drained minced clams, save half the juice. Mix in remaining ingredients and then add the juice.
3. Bake in 350° oven for 20 minutes.

Serve hot with crackers and a spreader (or with cocktail forks on a plate).

Make in morning and refrigerate until late in afternoon before baking.

Oysters Olympia

Serves 8

2 dozen large fresh oysters
½ cup butter
¼ cup minced chives
1 teaspoon summer savory

⅛ teaspoon pepper
⅛ teaspoon salt
2 teaspoons lemon juice
8 thin slices hot, buttered toast

1. Drain oysters well.
2. Melt-butter and sprinkle in chives, savory, pepper, salt and lemon juice. Remove from heat and let stand 5 minutes.
3. Reheat and add oysters. Simmer over low heat until edges of oysters begin to curl.
4. Place on toast and spoon sauce over.

Scallops Polonaise

Serves 5 to 6

½ cup Madeira wine, dry
3 tablespoons lemon juice
Whole peel of ½ lemon
½ teaspoon tarragon
½ teaspoon onion salt
½ teaspoon MSG
2 pounds fresh scallops
1 pound mushrooms, sliced

½ cup shallots, chopped
1 green pepper, sliced
1 teaspoon dehydrated parsley or
  1 tablespoon fresh parsley
1 small jar sliced pimiento
½ cup sour cream
1 teaspoon caraway seed
Salt and pepper to taste

1. Make marinade by mixing first 6 ingredients.
2. Place scallops in bowl with marinade; cover tightly. Marinate overnight, stirring once to coat all scallops.
3. Drain scallops, reserving marinade. Heat marinade to boiling. Poach scallops, a few at a time, in simmering marinade for 3 minutes. Drain thoroughly in strainer. (They will continue dripping.)
4. Reduce remaining marinade over medium heat to 2 Tablespoons.
5. Saute sliced mushrooms, shallots and green pepper. Add parsley.
6. Add poached scallops, pimiento, caraway seed, the reduced marinade and sour cream. Heat just till simmering. (Do not boil sour cream.)
7. Correct seasoning with salt and pepper to taste.
8. If sauce is too thin, thicken with a little Wondra flour.

Note: Serve from chafing dish with plates & fork. This so good that it will vanish. The same recipe may be used for raw shrimp. (Please note that although this is excellent, it is tricky, be careful.)
1. *Don't boil sour cream.*
2. *The scallops will continue to ooze over after draining. The amount of flour needed to thicken will depend on just how "wet" the scallops are.*

Shrimp de Jonghe

Serves 10-12

3 pounds boiled shrimp
1 teaspoon salt
1 clove garlic, grated
¾ cup butter
1 cup bread crumbs

⅛ teaspoon pepper
½ teaspoon paprika
Dash of cayenne
½ cup Sherry wine

1. Combine all ingredients except shrimp. Blend well.
2. Place alternate layers of shrimp and crumb mixture in a bake-and-serve dish, or in 12 individual shells. Last layer should be crumbs.
3. Bake at 400° to heat through.

The baking time will depend on the size of the container and the temperature of food when it is placed in oven. It is important that it be piping hot but not dried out. Individual shells at room temperature may be hot in as little as 8 to 10 minutes. A single container will require around 25 minutes to heat through.

Shrimp Supreme de Jeanne

12 ounce package frozen
  shrimp
1 onion, chopped
1/3 green pepper, diced
2 tablespoons butter
½ cup dry Sherry
  or Vermouth

½ cup cream of mushroom soup
Salt, pepper; garlic salt;
  to taste
1 jar cut pimiento
½ cup grated sharp
  Cheddar cheese
1/3 cup bread crumbs

1. Cook shrimp according to directions on package.
2. Saute onion and green pepper in butter. Add Sherry or Vermouth. Simmer till liquid is almost evaporated.
3. Add soup, seasonings, pimiento, and cooked shrimp.
4. Put in casserole. Cover with grated Cheddar and bread crumbs.
5. Bake at 325° oven until warmed through (20-30 minutes.)
6. Place under broiler till slightly browned.

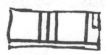

Seafood Kabobs

4 to 6 large 12" skewers
8 to 12 small 6" skewers

1 pound shrimp cleaned, fresh or frozen (thawed)
1-12 ounce package scallops, fresh or frozen (thawed)
1 jar large stuffed green olives
3 lemons, cut in wedges

Soy Basting Sauce

(makes ¾ cup)

¼ cup soy sauce
¼ cup salad oil
¼ cup lemon juice, fresh,
   frozen or bottled

¼ cup minced parsley
½ teaspoon salt
Dash of pepper

1. Marinate shrimp and scallops for one hour in Soy Basting Sauce.
2. Alternate scallops, olives, lemon wedges and shrimp on oiled skewers.*
3. Brush generously with Soy Basting Sauce before broiling and frequently while cooking to keep shrimp and scallops moist. Cook 2 to 4 inches from heat 2 to 3 minutes on each side. Broil just long enough to brown scallops as overcooking toughens them.
4. Serve with additional sauce.

* Skewer shrimp by pairing—turn the second one upside down and reverse its direction.

Serve on large skewers for outdoor grill or miniature skewers for hibachi. On hibachi skewers, they make "guest do-it-yourself" appetizers. If made on large skewers, they can be served as an entreé with rice.

SEAFOOD MOLDS
Gefilte Fish Mold

Serves 6

1-24 ounce jar of gefilte fish
in plain broth (6-8 pieces)
2 lemon jello
1 cup fish broth
1 -4 ounce bottle red horseradish

1 cup boiling water
1 tablespoon lemon juice

1. Drain fish, reserving broth.
2. Mix jello and boiling water; stir until dissolved.
3. Add remaining ingredients except fish; pour into greased 1 quart mold: chill.
4. When partially set add whole pieces of fish.

1. This recipe came from a friend in Florida—looks very pretty and tastes very good.
2. Put cherry tomatos in center of mold

Crab Meat Mold

Serves 10 to 12

2 boxes lemon jello
1½ cups boiling water
1 cup chili sauce
1 cup mayonnaise
2 tablespoons pickle relish
1 cup chopped celery
2-7 ounce cans good quality crabmeat

SAUCE
2 cups sour cream
2 cups chopped cucumber
1 tablespoon lemon juice
A pinch of sugar
Prepared horseradish

1. Dissolve jello in boiling water. Stir in chili sauce and mayonnaise until well blended. Chill until slightly thickened.
2. Pick over crabmeat and remove any shell or bony material. Stir into jello with pickle relish and celery.
3. Pour into 6 cup ring mold. Let set overnight until firm.
4. Unmold and serve with cucumber sauce.
5. To prepare sauce: Mix sour cream, unpeeled, chopped, well drained cucumber, lemon juice, sugar and enough horseradish to give a slightly sharp taste.

Suggestion: This quickly made crabmeat mold always gets raves. It has a crunchy texture. The sauce makes it especially delicious.
It makes an attractive platter with the green sauce in center of pink mold, and little mounds of black olives and cherry tomatoes and sprigs of watercress around mold.
Serve it on a plate with a fork in living room as an only appetizer. A rye curl or cracker is a suggested accompaniment.

Fish Mold (Tuna or Crab Meat)

1 can tomato soup
  and ½ can of water
½ teaspoon dill seed
2 packages Knox gelatin
¼ cup cold water
1 pound cream cheese
¼ cup chopped onion

½ cup chopped celery
2 tablespoons chopped
  green pepper
* 2 cans of 6½ ounce tuna
  or crab meat
1 cup mayonnaise
2 Dashes Tabasco

1. Bring tomato soup to boil, add dill seeds.
2. Soften gelatin in ¼ cup of cold water; add to hot soup.
3. Let soup cool 5 or 10 minutes.
4. Add cream cheese to soup. Stir until dissolved and creamy. Add chopped onions, celery, green pepper and fish. Fold in mayonnaise and Tabasco.
5. Pour into 6 cup mold and chill.

Serve with crackers or small bread to spread. Attractive in a fish shaped mold.

Salmon Mousse

1 envelope Knox gelatin
½ cup water
2 tablespoons lemon juice
1 medium onion
½ cup sour cream

1 cup mayonnaise
1 cup red salmon
½ teaspoon paprika
1 heaping teaspoon dill weed

1. Soften gelatin in lemon juice. Dissolve in boiling water.
2. Place in blender for half a minute. Add onion, run blender another half minute.
3. Add salmon, mayonnaise, paprika and sour cream; run blender another half minute.
4. Place in greased mold. Chill several hours or overnight.

For a heartier fish flavor, use ½ cup salmon juice instead of water; increase salmon to 1-15 oz. can; increase gelatin to 1½ envelopes or 4 teaspoons.
Serve with cucumber slices. Good!!

Salmon or Shrimp Salad en Geleé

1 pound shrimp or canned
  salmon, chopped
6 hard cooked eggs, chopped
1 cup celery, cut fine
2 tablespoons chopped
  pimiento
1 cup mayonnaise
1 cup chili sauce
1 tablespoon capers

3 tablespoons lemon juice
½ cup catsup
½ teaspoon sugar
1 tablespoon Worcestershire
  sauce
¼ teaspoon paprika
2 tablespoons unflavored
  gelatin
½ cup cold water

1. Soak the gelatin in cold water 5 minutes. Place over hot water till dissolved, mixing lightly and thoroughly.
2. Mix remaining ingredients. Add gelatin.
3. Turn into 6 cup ring mold; chill until firm. Unmold.

*(See page 26)

VIVA
VEGETABLES!

8

Antipasto

Shredded carrots (2 or 3)
½ cup sweet cocktail onions
½ cup green olives, cut up
½ cup pitted ripe olives
1 cup celery, cut up
½ cup each pickles,
 dill & sweet, cut up
1½ cups raw cauliflower buds

1 small can mushrooms
1 can flat anchovies
Tuna fish (large can)
 water packed
French dressing
Worcestershire sauce
Chili sauce
Mayonnaise

1. Marinate carrots for about an hour in enough French dressing to cover.
2. Add rest of ingredients. Use mayonnaise, French dressing, Worcestershire and chili sauce to taste to make the mixture moist.

No matter what you do it turns out great . . . !! Serve with party rye or melba toast.

Antipasto Riviera

½ teaspoon thyme
½ teaspoon rosemary
1 tablespoon whole cloves
1 bay leaf
½ teaspoon oregano
1 cup water
1/3 cup cider vinegar
2¼ cups tomato purée
1 teaspoon salt
½ teaspoon pepper

2 red onions thinly
 sliced (optional)
1 cauliflower separated into
 small pieces or
1 egg plant peeled
 and cut in ½ in. cubes
2 green peppers
 sliced thin
1—13 ounce jar salad olives-
 cut in pieces
1—6 ounce can pitted black
 olives cut in pieces

1. To make sauce: Put five spices into a *cheesecloth bag. Place bag in pot containing water, vinegar, tomato puree, salt and pepper.
2. Bring sauce to a boil and add remaining ingredients. Simmer 25-30 minutes.
A tea strainer is also a good spice container.
To your surprise, the vegetables will still be crisp. Can be made ahead. Refrigerated, lasts for a week.

Mix and Match Appetizer Salad

3 tablespoons wine vinegar
1½ tablespoons French mustard
⅝ cup olive oil
½ cup mayonnaise
3 inches anchovy paste
2 tablespoons capers
1 teaspoon salt
¼ teaspoon pepper
¾ cup diced celery

1 small cauliflower cut
   in tiny flowerets and
   cooked 5 minutes in
   boiling salt water
1—14 ounce can tiny
   artichoke hearts or large
   hearts cut in quarters
2 small potatoes,
   peeled, boiled, diced
½ pound cooked shrimp
   cut lengthwise in
   halves
1 pound mushroom
   caps steamed 5 minutes
   in ¼ cup boiling
   salted water and
2 tablespoons lemon juice
1 jar Belgium
   baby carrots

1. Whisk mustard with vinegar. Add oil slowly while stirring. Add
   salt, pepper, mayonnaise, anchovy paste and whisk until smooth.
   Add capers and celery.

*Just before serving, combine with any 4 ingredients in second
column.*

Caponata

1 large eggplant (1-1¾ lb.)
Salt
2/3 cup plus 2 tablespoons olive oil
1 medium onion, coarsely chopped
1-15 oz. can tomato sauce
1 minced clove garlic
½ teaspoon dried oregano
½ teaspoon dried basil

¼ teaspoon pepper
1 cup sliced celery (¼ inch)
1¼ cup pimiento stuffed olive
2 tablespoons drained capers
1 tablespoon sugar
2 tablespoons red wine vinegar
2 tablespoons minced parsley

1. Cut washed, dried, unpeeled eggplant into 1" cubes. Sprinkle lightly with salt.
2. Cook eggplant cubes in 2/3 cup olive oil over moderate heat until brown and almost tender. Drain on paper towels.
3. To same skillet add remaining 2 tablespoons olive oil, onion and garlic. Cook gently, stir often until onion is golden.
4. Add tomato sauce, basil, oregano, pepper and celery. Cover; simmer 30 minutes.
5. Add remaining ingredients and mix well. Cover and simmer until skin on eggplant is tender (approximately 15-30 minutes).
6. Cool, cover tightly and refrigerate.

Serve with crackers or Italian bread. Makes approximately 1½ quarts.

Eggplant Antipasto

Serves 12 plus

1/3 cup olive oil
1/3 cup green pepper
3 cups eggplant, diced (1 large)
1 chopped onion
2 cloves garlic
1 teaspoon salt
1 teaspoon pepper

1 teaspoon oregano
1½ teaspoons sugar
2 tablespoons wine vinegar
¼ cup water
¾ cup mushrooms
12 ounces tomato soup

1. Saute green pepper, eggplant, onions, garlic in olive oil in skillet.
2. Add remaining ingredients. Simmer 45 minutes.

Serve at room temperature on party rye.

It can be made ahead and frozen.

Poor Man's Caviar

Makes 2 cups

1 large eggplant
2 tablespoons oil
1 small onion chopped fine
1 garlic clove, minced

¼ cup fine chopped green pepper
1½ tablespoons lemon juice
1 teaspoon salt
Coarse ground pepper to taste

1. Slice eggplant into halves. Oil flat surface, and place them flat side down on a baking pan.
2. Broil three inches from heat 20-25 minutes or until quite soft.
3. Discard skin and mash pulp well with a fork.
4. Saute onion, garlic and green pepper in oil.
5. Add lemon juice, salt and pepper.
6. Combine egg plant and onion mixture.
7. Chill two or three hours before serving.

A low cholesterol spread.

Serve with crackers or some kind of chips.

Old Time Eggplant

Serves 6

1 eggplant-1½ pounds
½ cup chopped frozen onion
⅜ tablespoon oil
Salt and pepper

1. Boil eggplant in covered pot until it is quite soft when pierced with fork.
2. Peel off outer skin.
3. Chop in wooden chopping bowl until fine texture.
4. Add onion and oil. Stir and cool.
5. Add salt and pepper to taste.

This is an old Roumanian recipe contributed by a man whose father used to make it for his family.

It can be preared 2 days in advance. Serve as a spread with crackers at room temperature or cold. This can also be used as a cold summer salad or side dish vegetable.

Artichoke Hors d'Oeuvres

General Directions for preparing artichokes.

1. Remove any discolored leaves and the small leaves at the base of the artichoke.
2. Slice 1 inch off the top and discard.
3. Snip off points of the leaves with kitchen shears.
4. Trim stem flat and even with the artichoke base so it can sit level.
5. Rinse artichoke under cool water to clean.
6. (For 4 artichokes) Bring 6 quarts of water to boiling using a large kettle. Add 2 tablespoons lemon juice to the water to prevent the vegetable from discoloring. For a different taste also add 2 tablespoons tarragon vinegar.
7. Add artichokes to boiling water and steam for 30 to 40 minutes until artichoke is tender.
8. Remove artichokes from water carefully (use tongs or two large spoons) and place upside down to drain.
9. Chill artichokes for at least 4 hours before serving
10. To eat artichokes, pluck leaves one at a time. Dip base of leaf into sauce. Turn leaf meaty side down and draw between teeth scraping off meaty portion. Discard leaf.
11. When all outer leaves have been removed, a center cone of small light-colored leaves covering the fuzzy center choke will be exposed. Pull or cut off cone of leaves. Slice off fuzzy choke with grapefruit knife and discard, leaving the best part, the artichoke heart. This can be cut into bite-sized pieces and dipped in the sauce.
12. The choke may be removed before serving if desired. Open each artichoke like a flower to reach the inside and pull out the tender center cone of leaves, scrape off exposed choke with spoon. This is especially nice if serving as a first course at a dinner. The center cavity may be filled with sauce or dip.

Suggestion: Any dips or sauces can be served with the artichokes: lemon or garlic butter, Hollandaise sauce, or mock hollandaise, Thousand Island dressing, your favorite dip. See chapters on sauces and dips.

Stuffed Dill Pickle

1. Remove ends of pickle, hollow inside; invert and drain on paper towels until dry.
2. Fill with any cheese spread.
3. Place in refrigerator to set.
4. Slice into one half inch slices.

A tasty, easy, low calorie snack.

Tomato-Crab Bites

Makes about 30 appetizers

1 pint cherry tomatoes (25-30)
¼ cup low calorie
   mayonnaise-type dressing
1 teaspoon lemon juice
¼ teaspoon salt

A few drops bottled hot
   pepper sauce
2 tablespoons chopped green
   onion
7½ ounce can crab meat, drained
   with cartilage removed

1. Hollow out the cherry tomatoes. Invert and drain.
2. Blend remaining ingredients.
3. Stuff tomatoes with crab mixture.
4. Refrigerate.

This is a low calorie appetizer, about 16 calories per piece. Can be prepared ahead. Serve on lettuce and chopped ice.

Marinated Vegetables

Marinated Mushrooms

Serves 6 to 8

1 pound small fresh mushrooms	2 tablespoons prepared horseradish
½ cup olive oil	½ teaspoon oregano
½ cup red wine vinegar	½ teaspoon salt
2 mashed cloves garlic	Pepper to taste

* 1. Quickly wash mushrooms.
   2. Drop them in boiling water and simmer 5 minutes. Drain.
   3. Mix all remaining ingredients in a jar and shake well.
   4. Pour marinade over mushrooms, mix well and set aside overnight in the refrigerator before serving.

Can be prepared up to 2 days ahead.
For a quickie version of this recipe use ½ bottle Italian dressing for marinade.

Fresh Mushrooms Marinated

* 1 pound fresh mushrooms, cleaned and dried	½ clove fresh garlic minced
½ cup red wine vinegar	½ teaspoon salt
2/3 cup salad oil	½ teaspoon brown sugar (add more if needed)
2 teaspoons chopped chives	½ teaspoon peppercorns
1 teaspoon tarragon	1 bay leaf

1. Put all ingredients except mushrooms in a jar, shake well.
2. Add mushrooms. Refrigerate. Takes about 3 to 4 days to fully marinate.

Marinated Mushrooms or Cauliflower

Mushrooms or cauliflower
Japanese Rice vinegar

* 1. Clean and dry vegetables.
   2. Marinate several hours in Japanese Rice vinegar.
   This recipe is very low calorie. The Rice vinegar has a mild delicate flavor.

*

> *Cut off tough end of mushroom stem.*

133

Pickled Beans

1 can Blue Lake vertical
  pack whole green beans
1 tablespoon tarragon vinegar

Wine vinegar
1 teaspoon salad herbs

1. Drain half of juice from can of beans.
2. Add tarragon vinegar, and herbs and fill can with wine vinegar.
3. Let stand overnight in refrigerator; Drain and rinse off herbs before serving.

92 calories per whole recipe. Also good with beets, mushrooms or artichokes.

Fagioli Leonardo
(Marinated Beans)

1-7 ounce package Minestrone soup
  mix (beans only-no pasta)
¾ cup Italian salad dressing
3 tablespoons minced frozen onions
½ teaspoon oregano
½ teaspoon basil
3 tablespoons sliced pimiento

1. Cover beans with water. Soak for 3 hours. Drain.
2. Cover beans with fresh water; bring to boil and simmer 1½ hours or until beans are tender. Drain.
3. Place in covered jar with remaining ingredients.
4. Marinate overnight. Drain before serving.

This delicious vegetable keeps at least a week in refrigerator. It is an interesting addition to an antipasto tray or it can be served as an hors d'oeuvre with plate and fork. This bean mixture makes a good salad or side dish accompaniment.

Quick Cucumbers

6 cucumbers
2 sliced onions
¼ cup sugar
¾ to 1 cup vinegar

1 teaspoon dill seed
1 teaspoon mustard seed
1 teaspoon celery seed
1 tablespoon salt
½ teaspoon cream of tartar

1. Peel and slice cucumbers and onions.
2. Boil remaining ingredients together for 1 minute and pour over vegetables.
3. Marinate in refrigerator overnight.

ave
is

bil

_____ APT

_____ ZIP_

ks to re
U.S.A.

avings
$ 17.90.

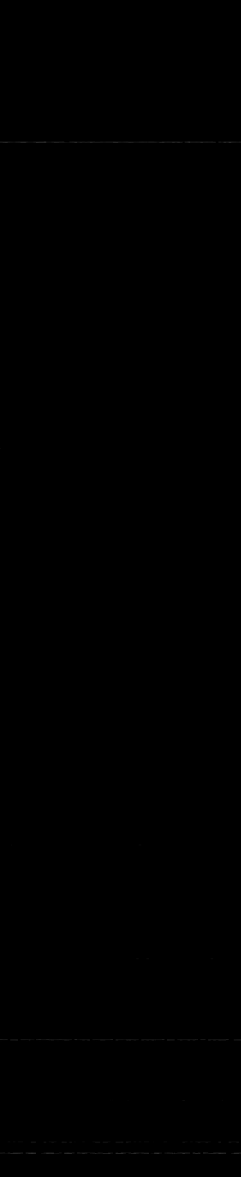

Brussel Sprouts Vinaigrette

1-20 oz. package of frozen petite
  brussel sprouts
3 tablespoons minced pimiento
2 tablespoons minced green pepper
2 tablespoons minced green onion

½ teaspoon salt
Dash of pepper
1 cup Italian salad dressing
Grated Parmesan cheese

1. Follow directions for cooking on package of frozen brussel sprouts.
2. Drain and cool. Combine the sprouts with all the other ingredients. Toss gently.
3. Cover and chill overnight or 1 to 2 days before serving.
4. Drain. Serve topped generously with grated Parmesan cheese.

Marinated Vegetables

* 2 cups mushrooms, cut up
1 cup cut green beans, cooked

1 pint box cherry tomatoes
1 sliced cucumber
½ cup Italian dressing

1. Combine vegetables with Italian dressing and marinate for a few hours.

Marinated Pimiento

3 tablespoons red wine vinegar
2 cloves garlic, minced
1 bay leaf
½ teaspoon salt
½ teaspoon pepper

2 tablespoons olive oil
2 tablespoons chili sauce
2-7 ounce jars pimiento
Anchovies
Ripe Olives
Lemon juice

1. Simmer first 5 ingredients in saucepan 5 minutes.
2. Blend in olive oil and chili sauce. Pour over pimiento.
3. Marinate 3 hours.
4. Drain pimiento. Garnish with anchovies and ripe olives.
5. Drizzle lemon juice over all.

Serve alone or as part of an antipasto tray.

Asparagus Hors d'oeuvre

1 bunch of fresh asparagus, washed and ends cut off
1 hibachi stick for every asparagus used
1 cup Green Goddess dressing
1 cup Italian dressing

1. Push the stick into the end of the asparagus.
2. Mix together: Green Goddess dressing and Italian dressing.
3. Pour mixture over asparagus and marinate overnight.

* *(See page 133)*

Pickled Carrots

1 - 16 ounce jar whole carrots
¼ cup chopped onions
½ cup low calorie Italian dressing

¼ teaspoon salt
½ teaspoon dill
1 tablespoon parsley
Dash of pepper

1. Combine dressing with rest of ingredients.
2. Cover and refrigerate overnight.

This recipe can be left in refrigerator for several weeks. Low-calorie.

Marinated Carrots

5 cups carrots (sliced or julienne)
   cooked, drained and cooled
1 medium onion
1 medium green pepper

Mix together:
1 can cream of tomato soup
½ cup salad oil
¾ cup vinegar
1 teaspoon prepared mustard

1 teaspoon Worcestershire sauce
1 cup sugar
1 teaspoon salt
1 teaspoon pepper

1. Cut onion and green pepper in rounds and arrange over carrots.
2. Mix remaining ingredients and pour over vegetables.
3. Marinate in refrigerator 24 hours.

Stuffed Radishes

1. Clean radishes. Place in water in refrigerator for 1 hour to crisp.
2. Hollow out center of radish. Cut stem end off flat so radish will stand.
3. Fill hollow half full of chive cream cheese. Fill up with caviar.

Red Radish

1. Carefully scoop out radishes with vegetable peeler, leaving firm shell.
2. Sprinkle with salt, and stuff with blended cream, Bleu or Cheddar cheese.

Celery or Endive Stalks

General Instructions

1. Wash celery or endive and drain on paper towels.
2. Cut into 1 to 3 inch lengths.
3. Fill with desired stuffing.
4. Garnish with paprika, if desired.

Variations for Filling Celery or Endive Stalks

Sardine Stuffing

1 can boneless, skinless
  oil packed sardines
2 tablespoons mayonnaise

1 tablespoon pickle relish
2 teaspoons lemon juice
Salt and pepper to taste

1. Drain and mash sardines.
2. Add remaining ingredients and mix well.
3. Stuff celery with sardine filling. Sprinkle with paprika.

Brazil-Nut Stuffing

6 ounces cream cheese
1 tablespoon grated onion
¼ teaspoon salt

Dash of Tabasco sauce
½ cup chopped Brazil nuts

1. Soften cream cheese to room temperature.
2. With a wooden spoon, beat cheese with onion, salt and Tabasco until fluffy.
3. Stir in ¼ cup nuts.
4. Fill stalks with cheese mixture. Sprinkle with remaining nuts.
5. Refrigerate at least 30 minutes before serving.

Peanut Stuffing

6 ounces cream cheese, softened
¼ cup creamy peanut butter
2 tablespoons cream
1 tablespoon finely chopped
  onion

½ teaspoon curry powder
½ cup chopped salted
  peanuts

1. In small bowl, cream the cheese and peanut butter together, using a wooden spoon.
2. Blend in cream, onion and curry powder.
3. Fill stalks with mixture and sprinkle with chopped peanuts.
4. Refrigerate at least 30 minutes before serving.

Spicy Bleu Cheese Stuffed Celery

1½ ounces cream cheese
1 tablespoon Worcestershire
   sauce
Chopped parsley

¼ cup crumbled Bleu cheese
Celery stalks

1. Mix cheeses and Worcestershire sauce.
2. Cut washed celery stalks in serving pieces and stuff with mixture.
3. Sprinkle with parsley and chill until serving time.

Can be made a few hours ahead.

Shrimp Stuffed Celery

1-8 ounce package
   cream cheese
Salt and pepper to taste
1½ cups chopped shrimp

3 tablespoons chopped black
   olives
1 teaspoon Worchestershire
1½ teaspoon lemon juice

1. Blend cream cheese with seasonings till smooth.
2. Add chopped shrimp and olives.
3. Stuff celery stalks. Sprinkle with paprika.

Stuffed Celery Tartare

1 pound top round, ground
   twice
Capers

Pepper to taste
1 teaspoon onion salt
Celery stalks.

1. Season meat with onion salt and pepper.
2. Fill celery stalks with meat, garnish with capers.

Pistachio Stuffing

3 ounces cream cheese, softened
½ teaspoon Worcestershire
½ teaspoon lemon juice
1 tablespoon finely chopped pistachio nuts

1. Blend cream cheese, Worcestershire and lemon juice in a small bowl, until smooth. Stir in pistachio nuts.
2. Fill stalks, and garnish with slivered pistachio nuts, if desired.

Celery Stuffed With Roquefort Cheese

½ cup Roquefort cheese
½ cup soft butter or margarine

¼ cup finely chopped watercress
Chilled celery stalks

1. Cream together cheese and butter and blend in watercress.
2. Fill centers of celery stalks and chill before serving.

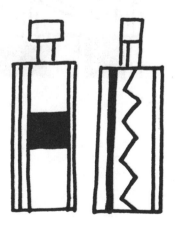

QUICHES

9

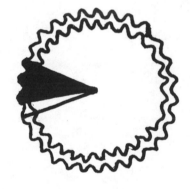

General Instructions for Quiches

1. Frozen pie crusts can be used to save the time of preparing your own pastry.
2. To prevent crust from becoming soggy, bake at 400° for 5 minutes before filling.
3. IMPORTANT: Place cooked quiche on a wire rack to cool for 10 minutes before cutting.
4. To prepare quiche in advance: Prepare crust as desired and bake for 5 minutes at 400°. Mix filling ingredients. Refrigerate both. When ready to bake, stir filling to blend, pour into shell and bake as directed in recipe.
5. For miniature quiches: Fit pastry inside small souffle dishes or individual tart pans. Bake 4 minutes at 400° or until very lightly browned. Cool. Fill with desired filling. Bake at 350° for 30 minutes or until set.
6. For a lower calorie quiche, substitute skim milk for half and half or cream in any quiche recipe.

Pastry for Quiche Crust

2 9" crusts

2 cups sifted flour
½ teaspoon salt
2/3 cup butter

3 tablespoons shortening
¼ cup milk

1. Stir salt into flour.
2. Cut shortenings into dry ingredients until crumbly and size of peas.
3. Sprinkle milk over flour and shortening mixture, stirring lightly with fork to blend. DON'T OVER-MIX.
4. Shape into 2 balls with hands. Chill 1 hour.
5. Roll out, using as little flour as possible. (Use pastry cloth and rolling pin cover to prevent sticking).
6. Place crust in pan, pressing firmly around edge. Do not stretch crust, but rather ease it in so that the crust doesn't shrink away from side of pan while baking.
7. Bake at 400° for 5 minutes. Cool on wire rack. Fill and bake as directed in quiche recipe.

Shrimp Quiche

1 9" pie crust	½ cup grated Swiss cheese
3 tablespoons grated Parmesan cheese	3 egg yolks
½ cup chopped cooked shrimp	¼ cup light cream
½ teaspoon salt	Dash of hot pepper liquid

1. Bake pie crust at 400° for 5 minutes and cool.
2. Place the Parmesan cheese, chopped shrimp and Swiss cheese in the pie shell.
3. Mix the egg yolks, cream, liquid pepper and salt and fill shell with the mixture.
4. Bake in a 350° oven for 45 minutes.
5. Cool 10 minutes before cutting.

Nova Scotia Quiche

½ pound Nova Scotia salmon	⅛ teaspoon nutmeg, or
4 eggs	a few grinds fresh
2 egg yolks	¼ teaspoon paprika
2 cups heavy cream	¼ pound Gruyere cheese, grated
2 tablespoons tomato paste	1 partially baked 9" pie shell
⅛ teaspoon white pepper	

1. Bake pie crust at 400° for 5 minutes and cool.
2. Beat eggs and egg yolks in a bowl until blended.
3. Add cream and tomato paste; season with pepper, nutmeg, paprika. Chop Nova Scotia salmon and add to egg-cream mixture.
4. Sprinkle cheese on bottom pie shell and pour in salmon-cream mixture. Bake 25 to 30 minutes at 400°.
5. Cool 10 minutes before cutting.

Crabmeat Quiche

½ cup mayonnaise	8 ounces natural Swiss
2 tablespoons flour	cheese, grated
2 beaten eggs	1/3 cup sliced green onions
½ cup milk	2 tablespoons butter
* 6 oz. can crab meat, drained and flaked	1-9" pie shell

1. Bake pie crust at 400° for 5 minutes and cool.
2. Combine mayonnaise, flour, eggs and milk; mix until blended.
3. Sauté onions in butter.
4. Stir in crabmeat, cheese and green onions.
5. Pour into pastry-lined plate.
6. Bake at 350° for 40 to 45 minutes.

*(See page 26)

Tomato Quiche

1 package (10 oz.) piecrust mix (or make your own 13" pie crust)
2 ripe tomatoes or 1 can (14 oz.) salad style tomatoes, drained
1 egg white, slightly beaten
3 eggs
2 Tablespoons butter or margarine
1½ teaspoons salt
½ cup + 1 tablespoon grated Gruyere or Swiss cheese
3 cups heavy cream

1. Prepare piecrust mix as label directs. Use only ¾ of the pastry; freeze the rest for something else.
2. On a lightly floured surface or between two sheets of waxed paper, roll out a 13" circle. Line sides and bottom of a 9" spring form or souffle dish. Pastry should come up about 2 inches on sides.
3. Bake pie crust at 400° for 5 minutes and cool.
4. Scald tomatoes if you are using fresh ones and peel skin off and remove seeds. Chop coarsely. Drain on paper towels.
5. Brush bottom of pastry shell very lightly with some slightly beaten egg white.
6. In medium bowl, combine the 3 eggs, cream, butter and salt. Beat until thoroughly combined—do not beat too hard. Stir in ½ cup grated cheese.
7. Put a layer of tomatoes in pie shell. Pour cheese filling into shell and sprinkle top with 1 tablespoon cheese.
8. Bake 55 minutes in 375° oven, until golden brown.
9. Cool 5 to 10 minutes and then loosen edge of pastry from side of pan. Remove side from springform. Place bottom of pan on serving plate and serve warm.
   If baked in souffle dish it is not necessary to remove quiche.

Swiss Spinach Quiche

1-8 oz. can refrigerator crescent
   roll dough
1-8 ounce package natural Swiss
   cheese slices, cut into thin strips
½ cup grated Parmesan cheese
3 tablespoons flour
1¼ cup milk

4 eggs, beaten slightly
¼ teaspoon salt
⅛ teaspoon pepper
⅛ teaspoon nutmeg
1-10 ounce package frozen
   chopped spinach

* 1. Separate crescent dough into large rectangles; place in bottom of greased 13 x 9 casserole in single layer. Press and seal holes. Cover bottom of casserole and ¼ inch up the sides.
2. In mixing bowl, toss cheeses with flour.
3. Combine milk, eggs and seasonings. Mix with cheeses.
4. Stir in cooked, thoroughly drained spinach (press out moisture).
5. Pour into crescent dough crust; bake 50 minutes at 350°.

Note: Cut into small squares. Serve warm. Can be frozen already baked and then reheated.

* *A pastry crust may be substituted.*

Quiche Lorraine

Serves 6 as main dish
10-12 for appetizer

Pastry for a deep dish 9"pie
   or a 10" quiche dish
8-12 slices bacon (about ½ lb.)
½ pound Swiss or Gruyére
   cheese, shredded
4 eggs, beaten
1 tablespoon enriched flour
½ teaspoon salt

½ teaspoon celery salt
¼ teaspoon cayenne
¼ teaspoon nutmeg
2 cups light cream
1 cup chopped onion
2 tablespoons butter

1. Bake pastry at 400° for 5 minutes. Cool.
2. Fry bacon until crisp; drain and crumble. Reserve 2 tablespoons bacon for trim.
3. Place remaining bacon in pie shell and add cheese.
4. Saute onion in butter.
5. Combine remaining ingredients and pour over.
6. Sprinkle reserved bacon over the top.
7. Bake at 350° for 30 to 40 minutes before serving.

(¾ cup sliced ham may be substituted for the bacon.)

Cheese and Onion Quiche

Serves 6 to 8

I 9" pie shell
2 large onions thinly sliced (I cup)
2 tablespoons butter or margarine
½ pound natural Swiss cheese, grated
3 eggs

I tablespoon flour
I cup milk
½ teaspoon salt
⅛ teaspoon pepper
Seasoned pepper

1. Pre-bake pie shell partially about 5 minutes at 400°. Cool.
2. In small skillet sauté onions in butter until tender and season to taste with salt and seasoned pepper, and turn into pastry shell.
3. Toss grated cheese with flour, sprinkle over onions.
4. Beat eggs well, add milk, salt and pepper. Pour over cheese.
5. Bake at 350° for 45 minutes, until knife inserted in middle of pie comes out clean.
6. Let stand 10 minutes. Cut in small wedges.

Quick Onion Soup Quiche

8 to 10 appetizer servings.

Pastry for a 9" pie shell
3 slices Provolone cheese
3 tablespoons dehydrated Onion
   Soup Mix
½ cup grated Swiss cheese
3 eggs

I egg yolk
2 cups half and half cream
¼ teaspoon salt
¼ teaspoon pepper
I tablespoon butter
   or margarine

1. Line 9" pie pan with pastry.
2. **Bake pastry at 400° for 5 minutes. Remove from oven and cool before filling.**
3. Place slices of Provolone cheese on bottom of pie shell.
4. Combine onion soup mix and Swiss cheese and sprinkle over Provolone cheese.
5. Lightly beat eggs, egg yolk, cream, salt and pepper; pour into shell.
6. Brown butter and pour over top.
7. Bake at 375° about 30 to 35 minutes or until knife inserted into center comes out clean.
8. Remove from oven and let stand 10 minutes before cutting.

SAUCES

10

Seafood Cocktail Sauce

1 bottle chili sauce
1 tablespoon horseradish
2 tablespoons sweet pickle relish
4 dashes Worcestershire sauce
6 dashes cayenne hot sauce
6 diced stuffed olives - med. size

2 tablespoons capers
1 large lemon, juiced
Good dashes of parsley flakes, dill weed, celery salt, paprika, lemon pepper, salt and medium ground black pepper

1. Mix all ingredients with spoon, seasoning to taste.
2. Store in covered container in refrigerator.

Suggestion: Good with crab, lobster, oyster or any seafood combination. Keeps quite a while. Does a good job of opening up your sinuses.

Sauce Louis

Makes 1½ cups

1 cup mayonnaise
¼ cup chili sauce
1 teaspoon Worcestershire
2 tablespoons lemon juice

1 tablespoon dehydrated onion
¼ cup chopped green pepper
2 tablespoons chopped capers

Combine and serve with shrimp, crab or lobster.

Remoulade Sauce

Makes 2 cups

1 cup mayonnaise
1 tablespoon pickle relish
1 tablespoon chopped capers
1 teaspoon chopped parsley or ½ teaspoon dehydrated
¼ teaspoon chopped tarragon
1 teaspoon anchovy paste

1 tablespoon Dijon mustard
1 teaspoon finely chopped onion
2 chopped hard-boiled eggs
2 tablespoons chopped celery
1 teaspoon horseradish
Dash of cayenne

1. Mix and let stand several hours before serving to allow flavors to blend.

Note: This make sufficient sauce to mix with 3 pounds cooked shrimp or crab.

Mock Hollandaise Sauce

Makes about 1/2 Cup

4 tablespoons sour cream
2 tablespoons lemon juice
3 egg yolks

1/2 teaspoon salt
1 tablespoon water

1. Mix well and put over water in small double boiler.
2. Stir until thickened.

Blender Mayonnaise

Makes 1 1/4 cup

1 egg
1 teaspoon tarragon vinegar
1 teaspoon red wine vinegar

1 tablespoon lemon juice
1 teaspoon salt
Few grinds fresh pepper
1 cup Wesson oil

1. Beat all ingredients except oil in blender 1 minute.
2. Add Wesson oil a little at a time.
3. Beat at high speed until thick.

*Mock Sour Cream

3/4 cup smooth cottage cheese
3 tablespoons buttermilk
2 tablespoons lemon juice

Few grains pepper
1 1/2 teaspoons salt

1. Combine above ingredients, adding more salt, pepper and lemon juice to taste.

A good low calorie, low cholesterol substitute for sour cream. Dill weed, basil or tarragon may be added for variety.

* *Mock Sour Cream can be satisfactorily substituted for sour cream to adapt many dip recipes for Low Cholesterol diets.*

TUREEN CUISINE

11

NOTE:

Whenever recipe calls for canned soup, this refers to an 11 or 12 ounce can unless otherwise specified.

SOUP SERVICE

The Butler did it—in the elegant past. But this is the era of do-it-yourself... so serve your soup with casual chic from mugs and a pretty ceramic tureen in your living room. Or dig out those wedding present punch bowl sets—perfect for cold soups.

Tip: For that extra touch that shows you care, serve cold soups in chilled mugs and hot soups in warmed mugs.

HOT SOUPS

Matzo Balls

* 3 tablespoons chicken fat at room temperature
2 large eggs
1/3 cup Matzo Meal or Matzo Cake Meal
½ teaspoon dehydrated parsley
1 teaspoon salt

1. Beat chicken fat, eggs, parsley and salt with fork.
2. Stir in matzo meal.
3. Chill in refrigerator for 1 hour or more.
4. Roll into 1½" balls.
5. Drop into 2 quarts boiling water.
6. Cover pot and boil slowly for 30 minutes.
7. Transfer matzo ball with slotted spoon to pot of chicken soup.

May be prepared in advance and frozen. Thaw before rewarming. Makes 8-10 matzo balls.

Matzo Cake Meal makes a lighter and fluffier product.

Lentil Soup

1 package dried lentils
6 cups water
Ham bone
1 onion, chopped
½ cup diced celery

½ cup sliced carrots
1 teaspoon sugar
1 teaspoon salt
¼ teaspoon thyme

1. Soak lentils in water to cover, overnight.
2. Next day, drain lentils. Add 6 cups water. Add all other ingredients.
3. Simmer, covered, about 1½ hours.
4. Before serving, thin to desired thickness with milk. Add hot dog, sliced.

It can be made ahead and frozen.

*(See page 108)

World's Greatest Vegetable Soup

Serves 16

12 cups water
4 large carrots
(cut in 1" slices)
1-3" diameter onion
(chopped coarse)
2-10" celery stalks, plus
leaves, chopped coarse
1 teaspoon salt
1 package Knorr's vegetable
soup mix
1 package Wyler's or Lipton's
onion soup mix

2-16 ounce cans V-8 juice
½ medium green pepper
(chopped fine)
1 chunk raw cabbage
(size of a man's fist)
chopped very coarse
1 teaspoon dried parsley
2 beef bouillon cubes
4 ounces uncooked extra-fine
cut noodles

1. In LARGE covered pot, bring water and V-8 to a boil. Add carrots, green pepper, onion, cabbage, celery and reduce heat to simmer. Stir frequently with wooden spoon.
2. After 2 hours add all the rest of the ingredients except the noodles and simmer for 30 minutes.
3. Add noodles and cook 10 more minutes.

Holler "Soup's on" and stand back so you won't get trampled.

This will make a gallon of soup. Plenty to eat and some for your relatives and freezer. As long as you're going to all this damn trouble you may as well make enough to be worthwhile, I always say.

P.S. You will have a lot of raw vegetables left over, so, in a large bowl, finely chop up the rest of the cabbage, and green pepper, 2 stalks celery, one carrot, one small onion, ¼ teaspoon celery seed, ⅛ teaspoon dill weed, 4 shakes Lawry's salt. Then pour one small (8-oz.) bottle of Marzetti's slaw dressing over it all. Mix well and you've got the world's greatest cole slaw.

Mama Helen's Bean Soup

1 package marrowfat beans
6-8 stalks celery, chopped
4-5 carrots, chopped
1 large or 2 small onions

1 tomato
¼ to 1 teaspoon salt
Pepper
A few shakes of paprika, optional
Large ham bone with meat clinging to it

1. Soak marrowfat beans over night.
2. Pour off water.
3. In large pan or 3 quart Dutch oven, bring beans and fresh water to boil. Jackets on beans will loosen.
4. Pour off hot water.
5. Adding fresh water to cover, bring to boil beans, celery, carrots, onions, tomato if desired, and seasoning.
6. Add ham bone.
7. Lower heat and simmer 3 to 4 hours. Season to taste.

Full bodied and thick.
Can be served in mugs before dinner or can be a meal in itself.

Cincinnati Chili

1 quart water
2 medium sized onions
  (grate fine)
2-8 ounce cans tomato sauce
5 whole allspice
½ teaspoon red pepper
1 teaspoon ground cumin seed
4 tablespoons chili powder
½ ounce bitter chocolate

2 pounds ground beef
4 cloves garlic, minced
2 tablespoons vinegar
1 large bay leaf, whole
5 whole cloves
2 teaspoons Worcestershire sauce
1½ teaspoons salt
1 teaspoon cinnamon

1. Add ground beef to water in 4 quart pot, stir until beef separates to a fine texture. Boil slowly for half an hour.
2. Add all other ingredients. Stir to blend, bringing to a boil; reduce heat and simmer uncovered for about 3 hours. Last hour, pot may be covered after desired consistency is reached.
3. Chili should be refrigerated overnight so that fat can be lifted from top before reheating.

Cincinnati Chili has enjoyed national fame since the much publicized Congressional Chili debate.
Serve it in one of the following traditional styles. There is nothing in any of these combinations that an antacid can't remedy!
Chili Plain
Chili and Spaghetti
3 way - *chili, spaghetti and shredded cheddar cheese*
4 way - *chili, spaghetti, cheddar and onions*
5 way - *chili, spaghetti, cheddar, onions, and beans*
Coney Island - *a frankfurter in a bun topped with chili, cheese and onions or any of the above combinations.*

Beef Barley Soup

Serves 8

2½ quarts water
1 soup bone with marrow
2 pounds chuck
3 scallions, minced

1 teaspoon salt
Dash of pepper
½ cup barley
3 ribs celery, diced

3 packets G. Washington's rich brown seasonings

1. Bring water to a boil. Add all ingredients except barley. Reduce heat to simmer and let cook about three hours.
2. Remove meat and bone. When meat is cool, cut into small pieces and return to soup. Add barley; let simmer one hour or more.
3. Chill overnight. Remove congealed fat.
4. Heat and serve.

Best when made ahead. May be frozen.

Oxtail Soup

Serves 8

1 pound lean stew beef
1 pound oxtails
8 ounces cooking Sherry
2 cans consommé
2 cans beef bouillon
1 teaspoon Worcestershire sauce
3 bay leaves
1 teaspoon Lawry's salt

½ teaspoon MSG (Accent)
1 teaspoon Beaumonde seasoning
1 bouillon cube
1 large can stewed tomatoes
4 carrots
1 large onion
3 or 4 stalks celery
1 tablespoon chopped parlsey
water

1. Put all ingredients in large size pressure cooker. Fill with water to within 1½ inches of top of cooker.
2. When cooker is at height of pressure, let cook for 45 minutes. Let cooker cool completely before taking off lid.
3. Remove meat and oxtails; cut meat from bones. Pureé soup and meat in food processer or blender.
4. Let soup cool completely, taking off fat.
5. Reheat before serving.
Freezes well. Serve in heated mugs.

Elegant King Crab Chowder

Serves 6 to 8

* l can (7½ oz.) Alaska king crab
l can condensed potato soup
l soup can water
l tablespoon freeze-dried chives
¼ cup diced celery

l can condensed tomato soup
l can condensed beef consommé
l cup light cream
Salt and pepper
3 tablespoons Sherry wine
(optional)

1. Break crab into bite sized pieces.
2. Combine soups and water in a saucepan and heat to boiling.
3. Add light cream, crab, celery and chives. Season to taste with salt and pepper.
4. Heat again just to boiling. Add sherry and serve in warm bowls.

Can be made ahead - add sherry when ready to serve.

Palo Alto Shrimp Bisque

Serves 4

3 slices stale bread
2 cans condensed tomato soup
l crumbled bay leaf
l tablespoon parsley

Salt & pepper to taste
2 tablespoons bacon grease
or margarine
l tablespoon chopped onion
1-4 ounce can tiny shrimp

1. Soak bread in enough water to soften. Put into fry pan with grease and all seasonings and cook briefly (as for chicken stuffing).
2. Add soup and equal quantity of water.
3. Heat, stir. When hot and ready to serve, add drained shrimp.

This simple version of a homemade soup has its origins in New Orleans.

*(See page 26)

Manhattan Clam Chowder

Serves 6

3 slices bacon, finely diced
4 cups boiling water
1½ teaspoons salt
2 cups diced potatoes
1 cup finely diced carrots

1 cup finely diced
  celery
1 cup chopped onion

* * * * * * * *

10 cooked fresh or 1-10½ oz. can clams, finely chopped
¾ cup strained clam juice
1 cup stewed canned
  tomatoes

½ teaspoon thyme
¼ teaspoon pepper

* * * * * * * *

3 tablespoons butter or margarine   3 tablespoons enriched flour

1. Dice bacon and cook slightly.
2. Add boiling water, salt, potatoes, carrots, celery and onion, simmer uncovered 15 minutes or till vegetables are *nearly* tender.
3. Add clams and juice, chopped tomatoes, thyme and pepper.
4. Melt butter; blend in flour and carefully stir into chowder.
5. Simmer 15 minutes longer.

New England Clam Chowder

Serves 4

1 pkg. Knorr Cream of Leek Soup
2 cups milk

1 cup water or 1 cup juice from clams
1 or 2 cans minced, drained clams

1. Combine soup mix and milk. Bring to boil. Cover and simmer, stirring occasionally over low heat for 10 minutes.
2. Remove lid. Add water or clam juice and drained clams.

Serve piping hot in mugs.

Quick Clam Chowder

1 can clam chowder
1 can minced clams
1 can sliced mushrooms

1 teaspoon MSG
Salt and pepper

1. Pour mushroom juice and clam juice in empty chowder can. Fill with Half and Half cereal milk.
2. Mix with clam chowder. Add MSG and salt and pepper to taste. Heat just to boiling point.

Serve immediately in heated mugs.

Zucchini Soup

Serves 8

1½ cups chopped onion
½ stick butter
8 cups sliced zucchini
   or cucumbers
4 cups chicken broth

2 teaspoons tarragon vinegar
3/4 tablespoon dillweed
2 tablespoons uncooked cream of wheat
   or 2 boiled potatoes
Parmesan cheese or sour cream

1. In dutch oven sauté onions in butter till wilted. Add sliced zucchini or cucumber, chicken broth, vinegar, dill, salt and pepper to taste.
2. Bring to a boil. Add 2 tablespoons cream of wheat or 2 cold boiled potatoes. Simmer 25 minutes.
3. Mix in blender till smooth.

Suggestion: A Vermont recipe. Can be made ahead and frozen. Serve hot topped with Parmesan, or serve cold topped with sour cream.

Onion Soup

Serves 6

2 cans Campbell's consommé
2 cans water
5 cups sliced onions
¼ pound margarine
8 ounces of cooking Sherry

2 tablespoons flour (Wondra)
1 tablespoon sugar
1 clove minced garlic
Chopped parsley
Salt to taste
¼ teaspoon thyme

1. Slice onions thin and brown lightly in the margarine.
   Pour off excess margarine.
2. Add the other ingredients and simmer very slowly for 2 hours, covered.

Make a day ahead. Remove hardened fat before warming.

When ready to serve, heat soup, place in bake and serve casserole. Cover with 6 slices of toasted French bread. Sprinkle with ¼ cup Parmesan and 3/4 Cup grated Gruyére cheese. Heat in 275° oven until cheese melts - about 5 minutes.
To prevent cracking, casserole should be at room temperature before placing in oven.

Split Pea Soup

1 pound green split peas
3 quarts water
1 medium onion, chopped
½ raw carrot, diced

½ cup raw, diced potato
1 ham bone or
⅛ pound salt pork

1. Rinse peas. Place in kettle with rest of ingredients.
2. Bring to a boil and let simmer for about 3 hours. Season to taste. Add more water from time to time, if necessary.
2. Put through sieve, reheat and serve.

Minestrone

1 package Minestrone soup
   mix
3 quarts water
1 ham bone
1 clove garlic
½ pound fresh spinach

3 tablespoons dehydrated onion
3 cups tomatoes
   (or large can)
1 teaspoon MSG

1. Soak Minestrone soup mix overnight in water.
2. Add ham bone, garlic, onion, tomatoes and MSG. Cook several hours or until beans are tender. Correct seasoning.
3. When ready to serve, add spinach and cook 10 minutes.

Suggestion: Serve with fresh grated Parmesan cheese.
This soup freezes well. Add spinach when ready to serve to preserve bright color.

Soup Italiano

1 can condensed green pea soup
1 can condensed tomato soup
1½ cans water
2 tablespoons dry red wine
⅛ teaspoon Italian herb blend

1. Blend soups, add remaining ingredients.
2. Cook over low heat for 10 minutes. Serve with Italian Rye Chips. (see page 67)

Almond Soup

Serves 6

2 tablespoons melted butter	l cup finely chopped almonds
2 tablespoons cornstarch	2 tbsp. finely chopped watercress leaves
3 cans chicken broth (5¼ cups)	Salt and pepper to taste
l cup heavy cream	Almond extract to taste (½-l tsp.)

1. Blend butter and cornstarch together until smooth. Stir in ½ cup chicken broth.
2. Heat remaining chicken broth and gradually stir into butter mixture.
3. Simmer soup for 5 minutes, stirring often.
4. Remove from heat and add cream and almonds. Allow to stand for 30 minutes for flavors to blend.
5. To serve-reheat soup. Add watercress, salt, pepper, and almond extract.

Can be made early in day and reheated.

Canadian Cheese Soup

Serves 4-6

½ stick butter	3 cups milk
l small minced onion	¼ teaspoon Tabasco
l large diced carrot	Garlic Salt
½ cup chopped celery	2 cups shredded Black Diamond
l cup chicken broth	Cheddar Cheese
2 tablespoons flour	

1. Saute onion in butter till slightly soft. Add carrot, celery, and chicken broth; cover and simmer 15 minutes.
2. Put flour into 2 cup Pyrex cup and add a little milk; mix thoroughly and fill to 2 cup mark, stirring till blended.
3. Add to soup; heat and stir till boiling and thickened.
4. 'Add cheese. Stir over low heat till melted. Season to taste with Tabasco and garlic salt.
5. Let set, off heat. When ready to serve, add l cup milk and more chicken broth to taste. Reheat to just below boiling point before serving.
6. Sprinkle with chopped parsley. Serve with garlic toast points.

Egg Drop Soup

Serves 4

6 cups chicken soup
½ teaspoon sugar
½ teaspoon salt
Dash pepper
½ teaspoon MSG

1½ tablespoons cornstarch
¼ cup cold water

1 beaten egg

1. Combine first five ingredients in sauce pan; bring to boil and simmer 5 minutes.
2. Combine cornstarch and water, add to soup and stir well. Add beaten egg slowly.
3. Remove from heat. Stir and serve hot.

It's not a sin to use canned chicken soup!

Wonton Soup

*6 uncooked filled wontons
1 can chicken broth
  or chicken stock
1 can water
1 tablespoon soy sauce
Dash of pepper
1 tablespoon green onion chopped

1 teaspoon sesame oil
Spinach, lettuce or
  other green vegetable (chopped)
½ cup bamboo shoots, sliced
Salt to taste

1. Boil wontons in water to cover. When done, they will float on top.
2. Combine chicken broth with remaining ingredients except onion and bring to a boil.
3. Place cooked wontons in individual bowls and pour chicken broth mixture over. Sprinkle with onion.

*See Dora Ang's Wontons page 58. Prepare wrapper and proceed with filling instructions through step 5. At step 6 boil rather than fry. (See step 1 of Wonton Soup).

Blender Black Bean Soup

6 servings (small bowls)

1 cup black beans
2 cups water
⅛ teaspoon mace
1 carrot, cut in pieces
1 onion, cut in pieces
6 cups water
1 small ham bone or ⅛ pound salt pork
¼ pound beef stew meat, cut in small pieces

2 cloves
2 hard cooked eggs, sliced thin
Dash red pepper
2 tablespoons sherry
  or lemon juice
½ lemon, sliced thin

1. Wash beans, cover with 2 cups water and soak overnight. In the morning drain water and discard.
2. Put carrot, onion and 2 cups water in blender container, cover and process at high speed on and off quickly several times to chop vegetables coarsely.
3. Pour into large saucepan. Add beans and remaining water, meat and seasoning. Cover and cook slowly about 3 hours or until beans are very soft.
4. Remove meat and cloves. Cool soup slightly.
5. Pour soup through a strainer, reserving stock.
6. Put vegetables into blender container, add stock to cover. Cover container and process at low speed to start, then turn control to high and process until smooth.
7. If mixture is too thick, add a little stock. Return pureed mixture, meat and reserved stock to soup kettle, add Sherry and reheat.

Place in tureen; top with eggs and lemon.

This is very rich, and thick and a little goes a long way.
*For low cholesterol soup use egg whites **only** as garnish.*

165

COLD SOUPS

Cold Purée Mongol

2 cans cream of tomato soup
2 cans beef consommé
2 cans split pea soup
2 soup cans milk
1 tablespoon grated onion

2 teaspoons allspice
Dash of curry powder
Chopped parsley
Sour cream
Seasoned croutons

1. Mix undiluted soups, milk, onion, allspice and curry powder with beater till well blended.
2. Chill in refrigerator several hours.
3. Serve in chilled mugs. Top with parsley, sour cream and croutons.

Quick Senegalese

Serves 4

1 can cream of chicken soup
1 can milk
1 cup chopped ice

½ teaspoon curry powder
Chives

1. Into the electric blender put the soup, milk and curry powder. Blend 10 to 15 seconds.
2. Add the ice and blend another 10 seconds or until blended.

Serve garnished with chopped chives in chilled mugs.

Smartini

1 can condensed cream
    of celery soup
1 soup can cracked ice

¼ cup chopped cucumbers,
    or to taste
¼ cup sour cream,
    or to taste

1. Combine all in blender and whirl smooth.
2. Sprinkle with dill for garnish if desired.

This is a quickie summer soup that tastes similar to vichyssoise. It makes a nice cool drink as appetizer for a summer meal.
Can be served in frosted glass with an olive.

Chlodnik

Serves 6-8

½ bunch green onions
½ green pepper
1 cucumber, peeled & seeded
1 zucchini
¼ cup celery, chopped
¼ cup parsley, chopped
¼ cup watercress, chopped
½ cup dill pickle, chopped

¼ cup dill pickle juice
½ cup yogurt
1 quart buttermilk
1 teaspoon salt
1 teaspoon dill weed
Dash of garlic powder and
    black pepper
* 2 cups shrimp or lump crabmeat

1. Mix all ingredients except seafood.
2. Run in batches in blender until smooth.
3. Chill thoroughly.
4. Just before serving, add 2 cups of tiny shrimp or lump crabmeat.

An unusual cold low calorie soup.

Make a day ahead.

Serve from attractive tureen in chilled mugs in living room as first course.

Frosted Crab Soup

Serves 6

2 cans cream of vichyssoise
soup

* 1 can crab meat (6 ounce)

1. Mix soup and drained crab meat.
2. Chill until ready to serve.

Make ahead. Place in chilled cream soup dish or mug. This is an easy substitute for the famous frosted crab soup, served at The Suburban Club, Baltimore, Md.

4 cups vichyssoise (p. 171) can be substituted

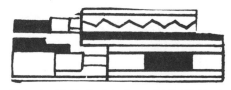

*(See page 26)

Chilled Avocado Soup

Serves 4 to 6

1 large, ripe avocado
2 cans clear consommé madrilene
1 cup dairy sour cream

Salt, chili powder and cayenne
   to taste
Grated onion
Minced fresh dill or crushed
   dillseed

1. Peel avocado and remove seed. Whirl until smooth in electric blender or put through sieve or food mill.
2. Mix with consommé and sour cream.
3. Season with salt, chili powder, cayenne and onion.
4. Chill until mixture jells.

Serve in mugs or bouillon cups with garnish of dill.
Can be made a day ahead.

Watercress Soup

Serves 12

1/3 cup minced onion
3 tablespoons melted butter
3-4 cups watercress with stems
   (tightly packed)

½ teaspoon salt
3 tablespoons flour
5½ cups chicken broth
½ cup whipping cream
2 egg yolks

1. Saute onions in butter until tender but not brown. Stir in watercress and salt and cook slowly until tender, about 5 minutes.
2. Blend in blender with ½ Cup chicken broth.
3. Stir flour into watercress mixture. Add chicken broth and bring to boiling point, stirring occasionally to prevent lumps. Simmer five minutes.
4. Correct seasonings, and stir in whipping cream, into which egg yolks have been beaten.
5. Place saucepan over heat for a few minutes, simmer but don't boil. Cool and refrigerate.

Garnish with unsweetened whipped cream and watercress sprigs and serve in chilled mugs. To serve hot, garnish with croutons.

Gazpacho I

1-46 ounce can tomato juice
½ cup chopped green onions
1 cup chopped green pepper
1-2 cups cubed, peeled tomatoes
⅛ teaspoon cayenne pepper

1-2 tablespoons salad oil
1 cup peeled, diced cucumber
1 cup diced celery
½ cup chopped parsley
⅛ teaspoon garlic salt

Mix all together and refrigerate.

Refreshing and delicious. Add croutons when serving (optional.) Can be made day before serving. Good to keep in "frig" during summer.

Gazpacho II

Serves 8

1 clove garlic
2 tablespoons salad oil
2 medium onions, chopped
1 green pepper, chopped
1 cucumber, part-peeled
   and chopped
4 stalks celery, chopped
1 handful of fresh dill, chopped, or parsley

3 medium tomatoes, skinned
   and chopped
2 teaspoons salt
1 teaspoon freshly ground pepper
½ cup any vinegar
2 teaspoons Worcestershire sauce
3 cups tomato juice

1. Press garlic into large bowl. Stir in oil.
2. Chop vegetables with sharp knife (not by machine), and add them to the oil as they are being chopped.
3. Stir in seasonings, vinegar and tomato juice.
4. Cover tightly and refrigerate for use the next day.
5. Add fresh dill just before serving.

Prepare, store & serve in same pot (but be sure the lid is tight). Everyone always wants to know the exotic origin of this really refreshing, crunchy soup. It is adapted from the Cincinnati Enquirer.

Cold Bold Tomato Soup

Serves 6

3 cups seasoned tomato juice
¾ cup imitation sour cream
½ cucumber

¼ cup celery
Green onion to garnish
Whole ground pepper

1. Blend tomato juice and sour cream.
2. Slice cucumber and celery thin as possible. Add to tomato juice.
3. Chill soup.
4. Serve in chilled mugs or bowls. Garnish with onions and pepper when serving.

Suggestion: Serve in mugs away from table.

Fresh Chilled Tomato Soup

Serves 4

6 medium sized tomatoes
2 ounces salad oil
Ground black pepper
5-6 drops Hot Pepper Sauce or
   3 drops of Tabasco
Curry powder

2 ounces fresh lemon juice
Salt to taste
Onion powder
½ pint sour cream

1. Dip the tomatoes in boiling water for about thirty seconds; remove skins.
2. Cut up tomatoes and put in a blender at medium speed for a few seconds, until you have a coarse puree and the seeds are ground up.
3. Mix in the lemon juice and oil. Add salt (start with ½ teaspoon), ground black pepper, onion powder all to taste and put in the hot pepper sauce. Mix all together with a spoon.
4. Place in the refrigerator to chill for at least eight hours.
5. When ready to serve, mix a half teaspoon of curry powder and salt and pepper to taste with the sour cream. Place the soup in bowls and garnish by floating a tablespoon of the seasoned sour cream in each bowl.

This is a delightful summer soup and is similar to gazpacho yet it is more delicate and unusual. The seasoning of this soup can vary depending on the tastes of the chef.

Vichyssoise

¼ cup butter or margarine
2 onions chopped fine
3 potatoes quartered
* 2 cups light cream
1 teaspoon white pepper

1½ cups chopped leeks
or scallions, (including green tops)
3½ cups chicken broth
1 teaspoon salt
2 tablespoons chopped chives

1. Sauté onions and scallions in butter slowly until onions are transparent but not brown. Add 1 3/4 cups chicken broth, simmer 10 to 15 minutes and allow to cool.
2. Cook the potatoes in 1 3/4 cups chicken broth until soft. Cool.
3. Put vegetables and broth through food mill or smooth in blender to obtain a very smooth mixture.
4. Add cream, salt, pepper. Mix well.
5. Refrigerate over night.
6. Serve cold topped with chives.

Thin to desired consistency with additional cream or half and half. For a zesty flavor substitute 1 cup of sour cream for 1 cup light cream.

Easy Vichyssoise

Serves 3

1 can vichyssoise
Salt and pepper to taste
4 ounces chive sour cream

1. Mix thoroughly.
2. Chill.

Serve with an additional teaspoon of chive sour cream on top of each serving.

Instant Vichyssoise

Serves 8 to 10

1. Use two packages of Knorr Potato Leek Soup. Follow recipe on package for vichysoisse, substituting 2% milk.
2. When cool put in blender with diet or imitation sour cream.

Serve cold from punch bowl in chilled cups. Garnish with diced spring onions.

Cold Beet Borscht

Serves 4

1 can bouillon or consommé
½ dill pickle
1/3 cucumber
4 ice cubes

1-8 ounce can julienne beets
1 tablespoon lemon juice
2 tablespoons pickle juice

1. In blender pour 1 can bouillon, the juice and half the solid contents of julienne beets (reserve the rest for adding later), dill pickle, cucumber, lemon juice, spritz of sugar or Sweet & Low if desired, pickle juice, and four ice cubes. Blend smooth.
2. Add rest of slivered beets and chill.

Serve with mock sour cream in chilled mugs.

Beet And Buttermilk Soup

Serves 8

2-8½ ounce cans whole tiny beets
1 quart fresh buttermilk

Salt, pepper to taste
3 tablespoons finely cut fresh
chives

1. One can at a time, grind beets with all their juice in blender until smooth.
2. Combine beets and buttermilk.
3. Season to taste with freshly ground pepper and salt.
4. Let stand in refrigerator 2-3 hours.
5. Pour into mugs and sprinkle top with finely cut chives.

No calories - well, hardly any - and can be made a day ahead.

Fruit Soup

1 pound any fruit (raspberries,
plums or sour cherries)
2 eggs separated

2 tablespoons cornstarch
⅛ teaspoon of salt
Sugar

1. Heat fruit and an equal amount of water to boiling point; strain and reserve fruit.
2. Combine egg yolks, cornstarch and enough water to make a thin mixture.
3. Add to soup, stirring constantly. Bring to boil and cook 3 minutes. Combine soup and reserved fruit.
4. Add sugar to taste. Cool.
5. Just before serving, beat egg whites with 2 tablespoon sugar, a dash of salt and a little grated lemon rind. Drop by spoonfuls to float on top of soup.

A refreshing unusual first course for a luncheon. Serve in chilled mugs.

JELLIED SOUPS

Jellied Gazpacho

Serves 4

1 can gazpacho
1 package gelatin
  (1 tablespoon)

1 can jellied consommé

1. Soften gelatin in ½ cup cold gazpacho.
2. Add gelatin mixture to rest of boiling gazpacho soup.
3. When thoroughly dissolved, add 1 can consommé to the gazpacho. Mix together.
4. Place in a bowl in the refrigerator until set.

Only 29 calories per serving!

2 cups of Gazpacho (p. 169) can be jelled by adding one package (1 tablespoon) gelatin.

Jellied Madrilene in Avocado Shell

1. Cut avocado in half; remove seed.
2. Spread 1 teaspoon French dressing over avocado.
3. Spoon jellied madrilene into shell.
4. Chill until madrilene is well set.

When ready to serve, top with 1 tablespoon sour cream and a little caviar. Serve with lemon wedge. May be sliced in quarters when well chilled.

Jellied Tomato Olive Soup

Serves 4

2 cans madrilene
¼ cup chopped green
 olives

1 cup diced tomato,
 well drained

1. Chill madrilene until practically jelled.
2. Fold in well drained tomato and olives.
3. Pour into soup cups.
* 4. Top with 1 tablespoon Mock Sour Cream (page 152) and sprinkle with capers or caviar.

This is a mild, delicately flavored soup. For a more highly seasoned soup you may also add:

½ cup finely chopped green pepper
2 tablespoons finely chopped onion
⅛ teaspoon red hot sauce

56 calories per serving

Jellied Clam Tomato Soup

Serves 4

2 cans madrilene
1 can minced clams, well-drained

1. Chill madrilene until practically jelled.
2. Fold in well-drained clams. Pour into mugs.
* 3. Top with 1 tablespoon Mock Sour Cream (page 152) and sprinkle with capers or caviar.

48 calories per serving

*If you can afford the calories use real sour cream!

READY
AND
BREADY

12

Pretzels

1 envelope dry yeast
1½ cups warm water
4 to 5 cups flour

Pinch of salt
Pinch of sugar

1. Dissolve yeast in ¼ cup warm water. Add remaining water.
2. Stir in 4 cups flour, salt and sugar. If necessary, add more flour for stiff (not sticky) dough.
3. Knead until smooth and elastic.
4. Form dough into a ball. Place in greased bowl. Spread lightly with soft butter.
5. Cover with towel and let rise in warm place for about 45 minutes (It rises about one-half itself).
6. Pinch off small ball of dough. Roll between hands to form a 20 inch long, ¼ to ½ inch wide strip. Form into pretzel shape, wetting ends and pinching together.
7. Bring 1 quart water and 2 tablespoons baking soda to a boil. Dip pretzels, let boil 1 minute or until pretzel floats.
8. Remove with pancake turner and drain.
9. Place drained pretzel on buttered, foiled baking sheets. Sprinkle heavily with coarse salt.
10. Bake in 400° oven 15 minutes or until golden brown. Cool on wire rack.

(Suggestions: Pretzels can be frozen after boiling and draining. Apply salt and bake when needed. Great with drinks. Good with mustard.)

Beer Biscuits

2 cups Bisquick
½ cup cheddar cheese, grated
½ cup beer

1. Blend all ingredients.
2. Knead 5 times on floured board.
3. Roll to a rectangle, 4 inches wide and ½ inch thick.
4. Cut into about 8 triangles.
5. Bake 8 to 10 minutes at 450°. Cool on wire rack.

Cracker Puffs

1. Soak saltines in cold water for 20 minutes.
2. Lift from water with perforated pancake turner, allowing water to drain off.
3. Place on greased cookie sheet 1½ inches apart.
4. Sprinkle with sesame seed, caraway or dill seed.
5. Put a ½ teaspoon pat of butter on top of each cracker.
6. Bake at 400° for half an hour without opening oven door. They will brown, crisp and puffed.
7. Cool on wire rack.
8. Store in airtight can.
9. Reheat to crisp before using.

Party Mix

6 tablespoons butter
4 teaspoons Worcestershire sauce
1 teaspoon seasoned salt
4 cups assorted wheat or Corn Chex, Rice Chex or pretzel sticks

2 cups assorted—
  Sunflower seeds (shelled
  Toasted soy beans
  Pumpkin seeds (hulled)
¾ cup salted nuts

1. Melt butter in heavy skillet, over low heat. Stir in Worcestershire and salt.
2. Add 6 cups assorted seeds and cereals and ¼ cup nuts. Mix over low heat until all are coated.
3. Spread out on large cookie sheet.
4. Bake 45 minutes in 250° oven.
5. Place on paper towels to cool.

Garlic Cheese Breadsticks

2 packages breadsticks
¼ pound butter (more if necessary)

1 tablespoon garlic powder
1 tablespoon Parmesan cheese

1. Melt butter in skillet.
2. Mix in cheese and garlic powder.
3. Roll breadsticks in butter mixture or brush with pastry brush.
4. Bake at 400° for 5 to 10 minutes.
5. Remove to wire rack to cool.
6. Store in any tightly closed tin can.

NOTE: (Any other seasonings may be substituted for garlic and cheese.)

Roquefort Cheese Bread

1 loaf French bread
1 stick of sweet butter
6 ounces Roquefort cheese

1. Slice French bread thinly.
2. Mix butter and Roquefort cheese together in bowl.
3. Thickly spread mixture on slices of bread putting them back together in loaf form.
4. Wrap in aluminum foil and freeze.
5. Bake at 350° to serve very hot. (Bake in the same aluminum foil.)

French Bread Fantasy

French bread
1 cup mayonnaise
1 teaspoon Worcestershire sauce
3 or 4 scallions (chopped)

½ clove garlic
salt, pepper to taste
1 small Philadelphia cream cheese (softened)

1. Slice French bread 1" thick
2. Press or chop garlic.
3. Mix mayonnaise with garlic and other seasonings.
4. Beat into mayonnaise mixture softened cream cheese and chopped scallions (including the green part).
5. Spread on French bread.
6. Broil a few minutes.

Note: This can be made ahead and refrigerated. Broil when ready to serve.

Onion Dipped Bread

1 loaf Italian or French bread
½ cup butter or margarine, softened
1 envelope toasted onion dip mix
Parmesan cheese

1. Cut loaf in half lengthwise.
2. Blend butter and onion dip mix.
3. Spread on bread. Sprinkle with Parmesan cheese. Cut into finger strips.
4. Bake at 425° for 10 minutes.
   (Delicious and so easy.)

Melba Toast

1. Freeze a loaf of white bread.
2. Cut crust off one end.
3. Spread lightly with softened butter.
4. Cut off thin slice.
5. Continue buttering end and cutting off a slice until loaf is used.
* 6. Lay slices on cookie sheet.
7. Bake at 250° until dried out and lightly browned.

* *For a zesty flavor, sprinkle with seasoned salt.*

Rye Melba Toast

Party rye
Beau Monde seasoning
Butter

1. Butter thin party rye. Sprinkle with Beau Monde seasoning.
2. Cut in half.
3. Bake at 200° for 2 hours or until dried and crisp.

SANDWICH LOAVES

Riviera Loaf

Serves 8

1 loaf French bread
1 pound ground beef
1/3 cup grated Parmesan cheese
1/4 cup chopped onion
1/4 cup chopped olives

1 teaspoon salt
1/2 teaspoon oregano
Dash pepper
1 - 6 ounce can tomato paste
2 tomatoes thinly sliced
5 slices sharp Old English cheese,
cut in triangles

1. Cut loaf in half lengthwise.
2. Combine meat with Parmesan cheese, onion, olives, seasonings and tomato paste.
3. Spread evenly and to the edges of each half loaf.
4. Broil about 5 inches from heat for 10 minutes (Less for rare).
5. Top with tomato and cheese slices. Broil 1-2 minutes, just 'til cheese begins to melt.
6. Slice and serve.

Suggestions: Good on English muffin halves, leaving the cheese in whole slices. Excellent for midnight snack and coffee.

Sandwich Loaf or Ribbon Sandwich

Serves 10 to 12

1 pound unsliced white bread
*3 fillings (egg salad, marinated
  tomatoes, tuna fish)
Butter for spreading

8 ounces cream cheese
milk to thin cheese
Parsley, carrots and pimiento
  for decoration

1. Cut crusts from loaf of bread. Cut loaf into 4 lengthwise slices.
2. Butter each inside slice. (To keep it from splitting apart later when cut vertically to be served)
3. Make 3 fillings.
4. Spread one filling on each layer.
5. Wrap with moist towel and chill.
6. Soften cream cheese in mixing bowl. Beat cream cheese until smooth, add milk until desired spreading consistency.
7. About 3 hours before serving, spread on top and sides.
8. Decorate with flowers made from parsley, pimiento and carrots.

Suggestions: Can be made the day before and frosted just prior to serving.
* *For other fillings, prepare any of deviled egg fillings (pages 87-90). Adjust mayonnaise to spreading consistency.*

183

INDEX

186

ORDER FORMS

I would like to order _____ copies of IN THE BEGINNING
Price: $6.95 plus $1.00 handling
   Ohio State Residents add 32¢ sales tax.
   Outside continental United States add $1.00 per book.

Enclosed is my check for $ _____

PLEASE PRINT OR TYPE

Name _____

Address _____

City, State _____ Zip _____

Gift card message _____

_____

· ·

Please mail all orders & checks to:
ROCKDALE RIDGE PRESS
P.O. Box 37848
Cincinnati, Ohio 45222
(513) 891-9900

ORDER FORMS

I would like to order _____ copies of IN THE BEGINNING
Price: $6.95 plus $1.00 handling
   Ohio State Residents add 32¢ sales tax.
   Outside continental United States add $1.00 per book.

Enclosed is my check for $ _____

PLEASE PRINT OR TYPE

Name _____

Address _____

City, State _____ Zip _____

Gift card message _____

_____

· ·

Please mail all orders & checks to:
ROCKDALE RIDGE PRESS
P.O. Box 37848
Cincinnati, Ohio 45222
(513) 891-9900

ORDER FORMS

I would like to order _____ copies of IN THE BEGINNING
Price. $6.95 plus $1.00 handling
     Ohio State Residents add 32¢ sales tax.
     Outside continental United States add $1.00 per book.

Enclosed is my check for $ _____

PLEASE PRINT OR TYPE

Name _____

Address _____

City, State _____ Zip _____

Gift card message _____

_____

. . . .

Please mail all orders & checks to:
ROCKDALE RIDGE PRESS
P.O. Box 37848
Cincinnati, Ohio 45222
(513) 891-9900

ORDER FORMS

I would like to order _____ copies of IN THE BEGINNING
Price: $6.95 plus $1.00 handling
     Ohio State Residents add 32¢ sales tax.
     Outside continental United States add $1.00 per book.

Enclosed is my check for $ _____

PLEASE PRINT OR TYPE

Name _____

Address _____

City, State _____ Zip _____

Gift card message _____

_____

. . . .

Please mail all orders & checks to:
ROCKDALE RIDGE PRESS
P.O. Box 37848
Cincinnati, Ohio 45222
(513) 891-9900